THE DRIVE TO AIM HIGH:

SEVEN POWERFUL MINDSETS PROVEN TO GUARANTEE YOUR SUCCESS

AL KAMARA

For Basar! Embrace the Legacy Mindset!

DEDICATION

I dedicate this book in the memory of my mother, Miatta Kamara, for her wisdom and courage to send me out into the world.

Also, in the memory of my beloved stepfather, G. Marcus Kelley, without whom, I wouldn't be who I am today.

The Drive to Aim High: Seven Powerful Mindsets
Proven to Guarantee Your Success

by Al Kamara

Digital | 978-1-944027-17-9
Soft | 978-1-944027-14-8

Copyright © Networlding Publishing, 2019

All Rights Reserved

www.networlding.com

ADVANCE PRAISE

"Deep emotion and learning as Al took me on this truly fascinating personal journey of discovery and life challenges culminating in, what is effectively, an essential guide for us all on understanding and developing a conscious, practical and very effective mindsets in our personal and professional lives."

- Colin C Lovering ISM, Senior Vice-President of Enterprise Solutions & Advisory and Vice-President of British Romanian Chamber of Commerce

"I've just finished reading Al's book. I did so quickly, but I can tell you I did it with great appreciation of the depth and practicality of the wisdom and experience which he has shared.

It won't surprise you to hear me say that I totally embrace the mindsets which he identifies as critical to a productive and satisfying life: observation, possibility, resilience, passion, courage and persistence.

The way he sums it up with the "legacy mindset" says it all. From start to finish, his story brings to life the importance of what others bring to our life, especially the belief that there is no limit to what we can do and what we can give to other people's lives, starting with those closest to us. In that lies our legacy.

What makes Al's book so special and meaningful for me is the way he has embedded these principles into his own life, which is truly an odyssey. I love the way he keeps bringing back the earlier mindsets he has identified into the stories about the mindsets he comes to later.

Another great strength of the book is the way he offers the reader practical suggestions on how they can bring these mindsets into their own lives. He also draws very wisely on pronouncements and life experiences of other people who embody the mindsets he shares with us.

In summary, Al's book provides a highly practical, principled and personal road map to carefully consider as one wrestles with the question of what constitutes a good life."

- John Pepper. Retired CEO and Chairman, Procter & Gamble; Former Chairman, Walt Disney Company; Currently, CEO of National Underground Railroad Freedom Center

"Al Kamara inspires the reader to achieve what we call in the United States the American Dream. From the small village in Africa to the big city of Bucharest, Romania, from village to successful entrepreneur. Now it is a Romanian dream but better yet it is a global dream for anyone. Mr. Kamara teaches us about mindset. He proves the fundamentals of psychology. The brain can become a coherent, powerful, fully engaged tool for anyone who develops the correct mindset. This book demonstrates this truth. The brain responds to mind. The Brain responds to thinking. The brain is adaptable. The Mind restructures the brain. Change the brain by changing mindset. Al's seven ways to restructure the brain creates the physiology or brain of success. It is a must read for all".

- Jim Bagnola, executive coach, international speaker, author of Becoming a Professional Human Being: How to Enjoy Stress-Free Work and Personal Happiness Using the Mind/Body/Work Connection

Contents

Introduction 1

Chapter 1: The Observation Mindset 7

Chapter 2: The Possibility Mindset 27

Chapter 3: The Resilience Mindset 45

Chapter 4: The Passion Mindset 73

Chapter 5: The Courage Mindset 111

Chapter 6: The Persistence Mindset 135

Chapter 7: The Legacy Mindset 151

Chapter 8: Why Mindset Matters 165

Before You Go 175

INTRODUCTION

"We are shaped by our thoughts; we become what we think."
—Gautama Buddha

What are the chances that a boy born into sheer poverty in a village in Africa, who didn't learn to properly read or write until the age of fifteen, would graduate from a university, become a successful entrepreneur, and eventually write a book?

I know, it sounds like a fairytale, and, it is truly *my* fairytale.

I was born in a small village northwest of Monrovia in Liberia. The population at the time of my birth was approximately 73 residents. The county where my village is located was a center of iron ore and diamond mining until it was destroyed in the Liberian Civil War. But, even before that, it had no streets, no streetlights, no electricity, no roads, and no running water. The houses were built from red mud with thatched roofs crowning their tops. We had no schools or hospitals.

INTRODUCTION

As was the tradition in my village, my father practiced polygamy. Consequently, he had a total of seven wives in his life. My mother was his first wife, and as such, became the head wife of the family. She gave birth to my older brother and me. Later in life, when I revisited my birthplace, I learned that I had nineteen brothers and sisters, making us a family of twenty children.

But, I always knew I was special because I believed my mother who constantly told me, "You will become a big man." The English translation means, "You will become a successful man."

It was a tradition in my village for people like my parents, who had no formal education, to hold strong beliefs in prophecies or words spoken by the elders. The eldest male ruled the village and made decisions on many matters the families of the village brought forward to him.

In my case, the prediction about my future came from the town chief, the eldest man in our village. His proclamation regarding my destiny was more than sufficient to trigger an everlasting belief in my mother's mind that I would indeed become a success. She took ownership of this prophecy, which she began repeating to me at a very early age. I only learned from my mother later as an adult that her belief in me "becoming a big man" came from the chief, my namesake, upon my birth.

Those four words inspired me to become the person I am today. They are powerful words, not because they contain any special wisdom, but because they made me believe in myself. My mother's trust in this prophesy that I would be successful empowered me to work through any failure that came my way. Her powerful belief in me has created a series of foundational mindsets that enable me to explore, learn, develop, and constantly overcome the challenges that life presents to me - to all of us.

Over time, these mindsets became real and useful tools for me - tools that helped me excel in school, university, my first job, the start of my company, and throughout my life with my wife and my children. Many others throughout history have used various mindsets to their advantage. I have adapted my own in ways that have served me well, and through this book, I hope they will help you take them to heart. During my research for this book, I also discovered that a number of famous people have benefitted by letting go of "small mindsets," and, instead, adopting powerful mindsets that helped them break through life's roadblocks to achieve great success.

INTRODUCTION

Take Kevin Hart, the successful comedic actor, and what he says about how he broke through to success: "No matter what, people grow. If you choose not to grow, you're staying in a small box with a small mindset. People who win go outside of that box. It's very simple when you look at it."

Hart's insight implies that people choose their fates based on their mindsets. He has seen, as many have, that when you hold a small mindset you don't leverage the opportunities that come your way. This could look like you're living your life from a *reactive* versus a *proactive* mindset. In your work life, this looks like you're working to avoid losing versus working to win! But, you have a *choice*. You can get on the path to success on a daily basis. Using your God-given interests and talents, combined with hard work, why not *focus* on developing mindsets that will steer you to success? I know you have that potential and ability when you tap into big (rather than small), *powerful* mindsets. Let me show you how.

I've spent years identifying, developing, and implementing seven mindsets that will give you a unique toolset to meet and exceed your personal and professional goals. They are:

1. Observation Mindset
2. Possibility Mindset
3. Resilience Mindset
4. Passion Mindset
5. Courage Mindset
6. Persistence Mindset
7. Legacy Mindset

These mindsets have given me the courage and strength to develop my business. They have made me more resilient and better able to reject failure as the end route to my dreams. They have developed my passion for all that I do, and a strong belief that good results are bound to happen if I believe in myself. And they have helped me grow into a wise man, and together with my wife, raise my two talented sons, encouraging them to dream and believe in their abilities and go after their dreams.

This book invites you to tap into these seven mindsets, which can help you achieve your potential and meet your challenges head on, no matter where you live or what areas of your life you choose to focus on, whether it's personal, family, sports, or business. In each chapter, I will showcase one mindset and share how I applied it to overcome specific challenges. At the end of each chapter, I will offer takeaways for you to quickly implement that particular mindset. This will enable you to focus on an effective path to your own success.

There is no question that the seven mindsets have helped me meet every challenge in my life. I am confident that after reading this book, you, too, will be able to employ them in your own *drive to aim high!*

THE OBSERVATION MINDSET

Amos Bronson Alcott, father of author Louisa May Alcott, and a visionary leader in educational reform, once said: "Observation more than books and experience more than persons, are the prime educators."

It is well documented that children learn best in a safe and loving environment. It may not look like the one you imagine, but it can still provide the nurturing environment and relationships that help children develop into adults with great values and behavior. Children learn by observing and copying the people they love; people who are warm and nurturing, and/or the people who are important to them, like authority figures (in the family or the community).

Many times, children will observe the actions of adults without them knowing, and then they often imitate them. Further, if what these children saw has an emotional impact, it will stick inside their memory and later activate in their adult life, often without them even realizing the genesis of that emotional trigger.

In psychology, this is called *observational learning*. It's also called shaping, and modeling. It's being taught through the actions, behaviors, and beliefs of the people that the children love, those who care for them. It is not intentional. Children will learn this way naturally, without understanding or reasoning its impact on their lives.

This kind of learning will produce patterns in setting lifelong goals. Children will copy not only behaviors, but also values - ways to build relationships, roles in their communities, just like the ones that impacted them. It's a mixture of what they see, the explanations they receive, and the verbal language that will empower both the action and description.

Sometimes, children will copy behaviors of people of higher status, people they admire. The adults around them are the ones who will make the connection between what the children know, what they understand, and the new experience. They give it structure and context to make the experience rich and more impactful.

My Observation Learning

In the village in Liberia where I grew up, the elders pass on history through storytelling. This was also a major form of entertainment for the children, and I was no exception. I reveled in the regularly held storytelling circles. There I was, cradled in my mother's arms, eyes glowing with excitement, leaning forward to catch every word of the unique and always engaging tales.

These provided entertainment for hours along with their timeless wisdom. It was during these story-weaving sessions that I planted the first seeds of the observation mindset that I would use throughout my life.

Today, children are raised with information bombarding them daily. From TV, commercials, computers and cell phones, and information about the wide world around them - all of this creates continuous stimulation that leaves them little time to spend authentically observing, discovering, and proactively connecting in the world.

From this perspective, I was lucky. Poverty notwithstanding, the life in my village was simple, but it had a kind of serenity, with few unexpected surprises. Days passed by in the same manner, one after another. As a result, I had plenty of time to observe every little detail of my surroundings.

For instance, I learned through observation how to make my own toys and how to avoid all the risks and hazards encountered in my daily errands. Those errands included bringing fruits and woods back from the forest, and learning how to gather water from the creek while avoiding the wasps' nests and forest creatures.

Psychologists have demonstrated that, as adults, we are emotionally shaped by the tiny experiences and interactions we make in our first years of life. Like the great Greek philosopher Aristotle once said, "Give me a child until he is seven, and I will show you the man."

For me, the most vivid experience connected to those young years comes from my mother. She was the center of my little universe. My mother used to take me with her into the woods and to the river where she would wash our clothes. Or, we would walk between villages for days looking for traditional medicines when she or one of us children was sick.

On those long walks, she would talk to me and guide me in ways that would have a lasting impact on my life. Observing and absorbing her day-to-day wisdom, warmth, and soothing care enriched my life with a desire to look for deep, meaningful, authentic relationships. It's that simple. It's all about your exposure to stimuli from a caring parent or any person. Studies show that we tend to unknowingly be receptive to the same stimuli in our lives as we were exposed to in our early years.

Observing my mother, I became strong enough to go through whatever I encountered in life because of the love and the energy that she gave me unconditionally.

Now, looking back from my adult perspective, I see that in those first years I also learned a great deal about the rhythms of life, people, and commitment by observing how the elders of my village lived their lives and performed their daily tasks. All of these activities called for us as children to be very disciplined and focused on carefully watching in order to learn one or more crafts.

One thing I remember observing is how my parents prepared our farm for planting rice. Rice farming in the villages of Liberia was labor-intensive work that called for strong discipline from everyone in the village. The men did most of the farming. As a child, I observed every year how my father and the men of our village prepared the land at the beginning of the farming season.

This process began with the men manually brushing the land, cutting down the trees, burning the bushes, and clearing away the remains of the trees. All of this was done manually. When the land was prepared, both the women and men participated in planting the crops using homemade instruments, or by hand-sowing the rice seeds.

Before we boys participated in the farming process, we first observed our fathers and the other village men daily. By watching diligently, we not only learned the best farming procedures, but also absorbed the cultural values of this important process. Additionally, we all adopted a dedication to farming. For those who stayed, they committed to caring for the land to feed the men, women, and children, which was essential to everyone's well-being. Here, due to the observation mindset, those in my village kept their farming tradition intact.

Even as children, we played a very important role after the rice was grown. We were responsible for keeping the birds away from the rice fields. We did this by observing the birds from a distance. Our young eyes were able to spot a flock of possible rice-snatching birds much farther away than any of the adult men. As a result, using the self-made instruments we had on the farm, we were able to chase any destructive flock away before any damage might occur.

Our work of observing and scaring the birds away was a daily task, and very intense. Sometimes our mothers would join us when they were not so busy or were just taking a break from other activities on the farm.

Even though the experiences I learned from at a very young age in my village only registered unconsciously back then, they eventually served to build my strong values around family, friendship, teamwork, and commitment to something bigger than myself - the welfare and sustainability of my community, my village.

Learning by Observing Beyond My Birth Family

When I turned 10 years old, my mother decided to send me away to get an education to secure a better future for myself. Now, that I am a parent, I can only imagine what it must have meant for her to separate from me. I was her second and last child, and she gave me her all. It was because of her selfless act of love that my life changed forever, and

I took a different path, one far better than the obligatory paths of my siblings.

My first adoptive father, Alphonso B. Gaye, was a businessman who managed his own private firm in Monrovia (about 160 miles from my village in Liberia). He worked in partnership with several multinational companies in Liberia. Later in his life, he worked for the government as the managing director of the National Port Authority of Liberia.

As an adopted child, I was essentially considered a servant to the family. This was an unspoken practice for underprivileged children. In return for care and education I received, I was expected at age ten to assume a variety of responsibilities that included cleaning, dishwashing, shopping, and learning how to cook.

I had to do all of these chores before and after school every day. But honestly, I never looked at myself as a servant. Rather, I looked at this new family as educators who could offer me more insights as to how to live a better life.

Because of the observation practices I picked up back in my home village, I now turned my attention to learning as much as I could about my adoptive father's business activities. I was keenly aware of the success his work brought him and his family, such as his numerous fancy cars, each branded with the initials of one or another of his children on their respective license plates. This was a major demonstration to me of what a businessman could achieve, if he was successful. I also took note of his style of dress, as well as the apparel of his many business associates.

Observing the details of his prosperity, his examples taught me. From the beginning of my stay with my new family I felt somehow strangely in my comfort zone. Even though my life away from home was far from agreeable, I knew I was fortunate.

What's more, my observation of his lifestyle as a businessman inspired in me a vision of who I might become. I *knew* that to craft my own success I needed to be willing to work hard and emulate the way he so effectively operated in the business world. As an adult, I would follow in my adoptive father's footsteps, becoming a sales agent first, then a business executive, and later, an entrepreneur. Becoming an entrepreneur was my first goal in life, and one that I unconsciously established and later achieved.

School

Another door that opened up with my new family was my entrance into school for the first time. I was registered in the first grade despite being 10 years old. It was the first time I had ever seen a classroom. I remember my first year at school was one of total repose. I didn't understand much of what was happening, so I kept quiet, but I was keenly aware through observation of everything I needed to learn.

Although I paid attention and learned a lot, by the end of my first year in school, I was still unable to use that knowledge and express myself accordingly. So, I had to repeat first grade. But again, it was fine for me because the additional time allowed me to fill in the gaps in my education from not having attended school earlier.

Even though I didn't fully understand what was happening around me as I entered school for the first time, within a few years I was able to put together a new framework of my life. This enabled me to produce new insights from the solid observation mindset I had established then. This observation framework was the foundation that fostered continuous learning and growth throughout my life. It was the perfect mindset and provided me with a foundation for all the other mindsets I have developed.

Summary of the Observation Mindset

Diogenes is said to have observed, "We have two ears and one tongue so that we would listen more and talk less." The observation mindset is exactly that: watching, listening, and absorbing all that you see. It's about not making judgments, but rather watching and listening, as long as possible, to gain deep, rich understanding that you can use to dramatically evolve. It's about being *mindful.*

The mindset starts with listening and watching what others both do and say without judging. Until you have spent time patiently listening to the words and watching actions of others, you can't significantly benefit from what you observe. So, be patient. Take what you see and hear and store these away. Create a stockpile of knowledge, like a squirrel hides nuts, until you have gathered enough data to then develop insights.

Insights are hard to gain, but they are what gives us information. Over time, knowledge is obtained, which is the combination of experience blended with information. Then, eventually, as you develop your observation skills, you will obtain deep wisdom. This is the path where the observation mindset will lead you - to the place where your patience and persistence pays off.

In the professional world, the observation mindset further leads you to create ongoing business value. No matter how much data, how many numbers, or how many facts you gather, without spending time to aggregate, synthesize, and organize the findings from your observations, you will not realize the full range of insights you learned from developing the observation mindset.

Observing *how* others achieve success is critical to both our survival and ability to thrive, what I term *thrival.* By observing what others are doing to achieve success regularly, you can then leverage the best of what you observe. This is perhaps the most important part of the observation mindset. It allows you to leverage everything from the thoughts, actions, and career paths of other top-performing achievers so that you can develop your own unique, successful roads to success.

As I stated earlier in this chapter, as a very young boy owning little to nothing, the gifts I received in life started with the words of wisdom I received daily from my mother and my elders. With nothing in the way of receiving daily wisdom on how to live my life authentically and transparently, I realize now that I had one of the best learning environments a young person could have.

Through developing the observation mindset, I set myself on a path to embracing the simple and most powerful lessons life has to offer - the lessons of how best to connect with others, embrace their wisdom, and then integrate it into my daily life so that it is always there to serve me as needed.

As a result of my eagerness to learn rather than argue with my elders, I found my path to success not as rocky as that of others who resist their advice. Instead, I found myself constantly learning and growing. Even when conflicts came my way, I was able to move through them because I had stored wisdom from my daily observations as to how my elders handled difficulties.

Take, for example, Sir Alex Ferguson, who is widely regarded as one of the greatest football managers of all time. In his book, *Leading*, he credits watching and learning through the actions and leadership of others among his most valuable leadership practices. He shares in his book:

"You can see a lot more when you are not in the thick of things ... when you are a step removed from the fray, you see things that come as surprises - and it is important to allow yourself to be surprised. When I stepped back and watched from the sidelines, my field of view was widened and I could absorb the whole session, as well as pick up on players' moods, energy and habits."

When leaders talk less, listen more, and then intentionally watch closely what is going on around them, they immediately begin to see subtle yet vital details, nuances that enable them to lead more effectively. [1]

Albert Bandura, the David Starr Jordan Professor Emeritus of Social Science in Psychology at Stanford University, offers the following four stages of observational learning you can use to build this mindset:

- Attention to something that is happening
- Retention of what is happening
- Reproduction of what you saw

---

[1] https://idealog.co.nz/workplace/2016/05/why-observation-leaders-best-friend-and-7-ways-you-can-cultivate-it

- Motivation that sets the stage for continuous learning from what one has observed.

Working from this framework, you can begin developing the observation mindset to further your success.

Steps to Integrate the Observation Mindset into Your Daily Life

1. **Think of a time when you observed the way other people acted.** This could have been your parents, your siblings, your friends, or your teachers. What opinions did you form from your observations? For example, did they reach out to you when you needed support or protection? Did you observe your grandparents who always made sure they brought you treats your parents would not allow, and you felt special because they took the time to bring you your favorite things? Or in contrast, have you observed your mother and father arguing, or your siblings cheating at games? What did you decide you would do in similar situations as a result of your observations? What did you observe that made you want to succeed?

2. **Ask yourself, "What did I learn from those experiences?"** By learning from past experiences, we prepare ourselves for future success. We expand our personal experiences when we effectively and intentionally take notice of what is happening around us, from observing our surroundings and the daily routines of others to insights gleaned from people of great intelligence or who have amazing skills, like athletes.

3. **Practice mindfulness.** Mindfulness is simply a way of watching yourself, your actions, your emotions - the way you respond to others, or how you live. Becoming an observer of yourself means becoming aware of your feelings, your thoughts, and all the subtle things that make you, you. So many of our reactions and responses to people, events, upsets, delays, and actions are automatic. They "just happen," only they really don't. Every emotion is preceded by a thought, often so rapid a thought we deny we thought anything at all.

Once you learn to step back from your emotions and to search inside for your thoughts, you will notice them. When you recognize your thought about a situation, you can change it. When you change how you think about something, you change your emotions and how you respond to a thing. A mindfulness practice is a simple way to quickly develop the observation mindset.

There are many excellent books on mindfulness that can help you. It is not a religion or religious practice, although some people use it in their faith. It is a way of becoming aware or conscious about something in our lives. When we start a new diet, for instance, we become very mindful (aware) of what we're eating, how hungry we feel, and how we react to temptation.

4. **Start consciously observing people.** Once you have gotten used to watching yourself, begin to watch those around you. It's easier if you go to a mall, airport, or other heavily trafficked public venue where people are less likely to notice you studying them, or to care. Most shoppers walk around in their own little world. You don't have to do anything. Just watch. Who do they talk to? What gets their attention? How do they walk? Purposefully, like they have a destination, or slowly, like they are meandering with no destination? Your goal is not to judge them, but to sharpen your powers of observation. For instance, what

do you look for to determine if a person has a destination, or not? Can you tell who is waiting on someone, or just resting on a bench? Can you tell who is a young couple in love, or who has been in a long-term relationship? You will be surprised what you already know about observing people once you do it consciously.

5. **Solve a problem.** Many young children, especially those who are extremely curious, will take something apart just to understand what makes it tick. They may destroy a toy, or an appliance (like a toaster, or computer) just to see how it works. Don't scold them. They are developing their observation mindset. Work with them to ensure they have appropriate things to explore, and join them.

Being curious and exploring things through observation is part of developing the observation mindset. Another way you can do this is through asking questions. As children, many of us were curious about everything happening around us. As we grew up and people stopped answering our questions, we learned to either find out the answers for ourselves, or we stopped asking so many questions. The next time you are stopped by something you don't understand, Google it. Watch some YouTube videos about it. Observe. Learn. Imitate.

6. **Adopt the Golden Rule: do unto others what you would have them do unto you.** Learn to observe better by using your daily life as the lab for gaining the rich insights that the observation mindset lends you. So, for example, the next time you're in a restaurant, a bank, or a business meeting, or on an airplane, wherever and whenever you have an opportunity to observe the actions and words of others, *take the time*. Engage with those people. Ask open-ended questions, such as, "How is your day going?" There are immediate and long-term benefits to implementing this mindset. People who build relationships with those in their neighborhood - people you see daily at the store or dry cleaners, or in your office building - live longer and have happier lives. You are connected. Now you have even more opportunities to implement the observation mindset.

7. **Learn someone's name and use it to connect with them as you observe them.** This is one of the most authentic and beautiful ways you can honor someone. This makes them feel important. This also

opens up the hearts of those you meet, giving you much more to observe and learn from them.

THE POSSIBILITY MINDSET

"Man often becomes what he believes himself to be. If I keep on saying to myself that I cannot do a certain thing, it is possible that I may end by really becoming incapable of doing it. On the contrary, if I have the belief that I can do it, I shall surely acquire the capacity to do it even if I may not have it at the beginning."
— Mahatma Gandhi

Babies' brains are impacted more in their first five years of life than in all the years following.[2] During these years, parents play the most important role in their lives. This is a major reason why the possibility mindset can be taught at an early age.

This possibility mindset is all about believing you can accomplish almost any task, achieve

---

[2] https://www.firstthingsfirst.org/early-childhood-matters/brain-development/

almost any goal, and continuously create opportunities even when your friends, family, coworkers, and others tell you that what you seek to accomplish is not possible. The possibility mindset gives you the courage to grow, to really go for your goals even if you are fearful of failing.

The possibility mindset also helps you to accept the hard work it often takes to achieve your goals. The possibility mindset is like the kindling that ignites a fire. The base of this mindset is about creating the *expectation* that you will indeed reach your goals.

Fortunately for me, hard work was something I took for granted. From my youngest years, helping my mother with her daily errands and then keeping my daily commitments to my adoptive family, I realized that my hard work could translate into bigger possibilities for my life. I embraced that insight.

But, the possibility mindset does not look at why things *won't* work. Rather it looks at how and why they *can* and *will* work. There is an American story about two young brothers who both wanted a horse for Christmas. They are each led to a barn with two stalls. One received a horse, the other a pile of horse manure 10 feet high. This horse manure fills the stall. The brother who is given the stall with the manure is excited, and immediately grabs a shovel and starts digging. His brother asks him why he is so excited. The boy replies, "With this much horse manure, there's got to be a pony here somewhere!" The possibility mindset doesn't look at what *doesn't* exist, but what *can* exist.

Additionally, the possibility mindset helps you when a new idea, thought, or situation is presented to see a myriad of possibilities that might potentially be available to you. With this mindset you don't have to limit yourself to obvious outcomes. Instead, you realize and take advantage of many options. You *know* you will find that light at the end of the tunnel. You are open to unexpected, great surprises that can come your way when you steadily hold this mindset.

Accelerating Innovation by Using the Possibility Mindset

I believe it's possible to accelerate the progress of innovation through use of the possibility mindset. This is exemplified in a quote by Albert Einstein: "Imagination is more important than knowledge. For knowledge is limited, whereas imagination embraces the entire world, stimulating progress, giving birth to evolution." The reasoning behind this quote is that knowledge only informs us of what is *currently* the case, and therefore it is limited. Imagination, on the other hand, gives birth to what *could be*.

Another example of innovation being accelerated via the possibility mindset took place in the mid-1800s when the city of Chicago was challenged by an unusual situation with its sewage system. Chicago is and was at that time, a low-lying city, and therefore, water simply didn't drain out of it. Digging was not a viable solution as it would be extremely difficult and cost-prohibitive. An uncommon solution was definitely needed, but not readily apparent.

Fortunately, George Pullman, a young engineer who had the possibility mindset came up with the requisite pathway to solve this major issue. Rather than digging, Pullman found ways to elevate the buildings by the use of jackscrews. Then, when the structures were lifted, they added timber for extra support. Next, they constructed new foundations for the buildings prior to lowering them back to their original positions. The amazing thing was that this enormous undertaking took place without interrupting business in the buildings.

This incredible feat of engineering was achieved because George Pullman utilized his own possibility mindset, the ability to create, consider, and seek out new, and sometimes, previously unheard of and nontraditional methodologies.

How I Built My Possibility Mindset

When my first step-parents decided to leave Liberia for the US, I was granted the chance to remain in Monrovia with my second adoptive family. With the blessing of my birth parents, it was my big opportunity to move forward. This time, I had a powerful stepmother to admire, to observe, and learn from.

My second stepmother was Minnie Louise Greene, widow of former Liberian Vice President James E. Greene. I was the fourth member of my second adoptive family, as my stepmother already had three nieces in her care. While being part of my former (second) family of the Republic of Liberia wasn't included in the plan set out by my birth parents, it was a critical event that changed my life. Had it not taken place, my life wouldn't have taken me later to an unknown destination that had such a positive impact on my life.

Perhaps, I had been just lucky, or perhaps, as Douglas MacArthur observed, "The best luck of all is the luck you make for yourself." With their decision to send me away to get an education, my birth parents initiated my luck. Now, it was up to me to make the best of my next new family situation. If I were unable to do that, I would let them down and have to return to my village.

While living with the Greenes, one of the primary lessons I learned was to value education, always. The first house rule was that education came first. The focus was on learning. The second house rule was to attend church every Sunday. There was no playtime until we returned from church.

I was in the third grade when I arrived at my second adoptive family. Education being the most important requirement for my stepmother, I began taking tutoring classes immediately. During that year, I soon realized that the school level that I had been enrolled in was very low. I found myself actually *above* the level of my class.

I was not the only one to realize my own evolution. My teacher who had been with me from the first grade also recognized my development.

When explaining to him that I had moved to a new family and was having daily tutoring classes at home, he promised me that he would promote me to a higher grade if I kept up the hard work, maintained my discipline, and obtained good marks. Consequently, at the end of the school year, he promoted me to the fifth grade, instead of the fourth grade. It was a huge step forward for me. He had given me the courage to believe in myself and to see possibilities to advance in my education.

My Wise Stepmother

Besides the many friends and relatives that visited my stepmother, she also constantly had many important people coming over to the house. Later on, in my life, I figured out they came to seek advice, consultation, or perhaps to simply pay their respects to her. I used to observe her, admiring her manners and wisdom. I used the observation mindset and then enriched my awareness with the first seeds of the possibility mindset.

As I was observing and growing in understanding, this time I was also believing and working towards a better future. Having such an exemplary stepmother's footsteps to fill, I set *my second goal in life* - to become a *leader, a mentor, and a coach*. My stepmother was leading by example, and

I, too, wanted to become someone to whom others could come for advice, to consult with or discuss issues that most matter to them, or to simply share their life experiences.

Although I was a village child and the newest member of the family, I was noticed a lot. Why? Because I was grateful. I followed advice, and when asked to perform a task, I did my best while also being attentive to those around me. My duties in the house were fewer compared to the chores I was responsible for during my stay with my first adoptive family. This time, I mostly served guests whenever we had visitors.

Interestingly, it just so happened that one of those guests became my next adoptive father. I was responsible for ironing his clothes and shining his shoes during his stay at the house, which he appreciated very much, just like he approved of my attitude and manners.

For me, serving the guests was a responsibility that I took seriously, and I did it with all my might, heart, and consciousness. As Dr. Martin Luther King Jr. once stated, "If a man is called to be a street sweeper, he should sweep streets even as a Michelangelo painted, or Beethoven composed music or Shakespeare wrote poetry. He should sweep streets so well that all the hosts of heaven and earth will pause to say, 'Here lived a great street sweeper who did his job well.'"

With this attitude, I soon moved on to my next family, my third adoptive family and beloved stepfather.

Lessons from School in Canada

My stepfather, G. Marcus Kelley, was a diplomat. It so happened that when I first met him, he had just received a post at the Liberian Embassy in Ottawa, Canada. Again, as I mentioned above, he had recognized my positive attitude and follow-through behavior, especially with guests at my stepmother's home, so he asked if he could take me along with him to Canada as his adoptive son. I could not have asked for a better opportunity at that time in my young life. It was truly a unique chance.

We ended up departing from Liberia to Canada on the outskirts of the Civil War there. This was a true blessing. The move gave me a wonderful chance to study and grow my academic skills at an entirely new level.

Back in Liberia, my elementary schooling was short, as was my time as a child. I had been promoted to the seventh grade just before we left. I was now 18 years old. Remember, I had only begun to properly read and write by the age of 15. However, when I arrived in Ottawa, I was enrolled directly in the ninth grade, due to my age. This "promotion" unwittingly caused me to jump over two years of middle school education. Those two years are some of the most formative, foundational years that are deemed so important in the educational process, and yet, I missed them.

My new school was a trade/technical high school. Trade high schools are designed to provide vocational education. They give students technical skills required to perform the tasks of a particular industry and specific job upon graduation.

Immediately after school started, my Auto Mechanics teacher noticed me. I was different from the other kids, most of whom were from the Caribbean. However, it was not my looks or skills that my teacher noticed. My observation mindset made the difference. I was attentive, focused on everything around me, careful on details, and committed to results. During my first few months in the technical high school, I had a very positive attitude and was eager to learn.

Each assignment or classroom project was a wow for me. I couldn't wait to ask questions or finish my assignment and ask the teacher for another task. I was active, very observant, and completed all of my assignments with passion. After all, it was my first time having this level of education and being in such a great learning environment. Looking back now, I have a strong belief that I could have become a successful auto mechanic or run a business in the auto industry had I graduated from my technical high school. That period rooted in me a strong and everlasting possibility mindset.

But, certainly one of the biggest gifts I received by moving was the gift of entering a country filled with possibilities: culture, customs, and business practices. Canada extended the warmest of welcomes to me. One example is that after a little time and without my knowledge, my Auto Mechanics teacher noticed my work and approached the school director/board requesting that I be evaluated to assess my skills level.

Although I was very happy in the vocational school where I was at the time, I was very thrilled to find out that my assessment scores resulted in a recommendation that I be given the green light to move to a high school.

Up until that time in my life, this was by far my biggest achievement. It was a big kind of aha moment because the assessment results meant that I was academically somewhere above the level of the average kids in my school. This awareness served to motivate me even more to do my best at all times and to explore all *possibilities*.

I was determined and focused on learning, and now I had gained the opportunity to learn other disciplines in high school. I remember the smile across my dad's face when I took the report to him. He was so very proud of me, showing a greater deal of emotion than I could ever have hoped for.

He then told me, "The possibility was only possible because you *believed* it was possible." I'll never forget that. I was helped by a performance school system and given an excellent opportunity. I was prepared to work hard and make myself worthy of that opportunity. Furthermore, the mere fact that upon graduation from a high school I could attend either college or university opened a whole new world for me!

Upon moving to the high school, I spent most of my time away from home. I was part of the school's sports team and focused on track and field, basketball, and softball. We had practices every morning and sometimes in the afternoons, when I could stay to participate. Besides day schooling, I also had to attend night school in order to earn additional credits needed to graduate as well as to catch up on those missing years of schooling.

Night school was also important in order for me to improve my English and reading skills. You see, the school system in Canada is based on credits. Students need to earn a number of credits until twelfth grade before they can graduate from high school. It was definitely a challenge, but again, I was extremely motivated. I did not care about all the extra work and time I had to put in. I was happy to be so busy and thrilled to be learning so much.

My learning was accelerated because both the education system and the culture in Canada were so supportive. As Carol Dweck wrote in her book, *Mindset: The New Psychology of Success,* "Culture can play a large role in shaping our beliefs." For me, being in Canada helped me believe that everything was possible.

I made lots of friends at my new high school. My best friend, George, was born in Canada after his parents emigrated from Lebanon. One summer, George had a part-time job at a very big hotel, taking care of the parking lot. I remember visiting him one night and being awestruck by all of the beautiful, fancy cars he watched over.

I also loved being on the sports team of the school. The tradition of the school was to announce the team's performance as well as the best individual results each time we attended a competition. For me, it was all about hearing my name being read on the school radio, which I believed made me more attractive to the girls. Schooling was all about learning, growing and fun. It was such a great time in my life. This sadly came to pretty much a screeching halt, when I arrived home one night to find out from my dad that we were to be transferred to Romania.

I had never heard of Romania before. At school the next day when I told my friends and teachers about our upcoming move, I remember my coach asking me, "What did your dad do to your government?" He made it sound like my dad had upset someone from the foreign ministry, or that someone wanted to punish him. I didn't understand what he meant until we later arrived in Romania. It didn't take long for understanding to dawn on me as I quickly became aware of the dire conditions there.

I want to take a bit of time now to backtrack a little in order to share some of the historic events that took place in Romania around the time we first arrived, and for the first few years I lived here.

At the time we arrived, Romania was under Nicolae Ceausescu's communist regime. It was still a year before the revolution would take place. This meant severe austerity measures for Romanian citizens, and a massive decrease in living standards, such as food shortages that became part of our everyday lives.[3]

Also, shortly after we arrived in Romania, an extremely important and heinous event unfolded. It was the Liberian Civil War, which killed about 250,000 people and very well could have killed me if I had not left.[4]

The horrific war lasted for nearly 15 years, and many of the victims included child soldiers. More than half of Liberia's war-ravaged population was under the age of 18.

Around the age of 12, children were forced into becoming child soldiers. I still get chills thinking that it could have been my fate, too, had I not been

---

[3] https://rolandia.eu/romania-ceausescu-communist-regime/
[4] https://en.wikipedia.org/wiki/First_Liberian_Civil_War.

blessed to leave Liberia when I did. Of the 1.4 million children, it is estimated that as many as 15,000 to 20,000 served as child soldiers in the Liberian Civil War.

I knew that I was incredibly fortunate, beyond lucky, really, that I now lived in Romania with my stepfather. During the Civil War, Liberian children had no access to schools. Many basic needs weren't met. Coming to Romania without completing high school wasn't part of my perfect scenario, but I certainly had multiple advantages over those children back in my homeland. I was well aware of that and more than grateful.

I had been on a fast track in Canada with its perfect culture and superb educational system. Additionally, I had made many friends that meant a lot to me. Then one day, at the ring of a fax machine, it was time to move on to Bucharest, Romania. There, things would be radically different. I could have easily assumed that my destiny of becoming a "big man" was finished, but I had already learned through experience that I had to see Romania as merely another opportunity to fulfill my destiny. By now, deeply rooted in my mind, I had developed a valuable new mindset: the possibility mindset.

Steps to Integrate the Possibility Mindset into Your Daily Life

1. **If you have found solutions in the past, you can do it again.** Think of a time you found a solution to something that no one else offered. The goal here is to anchor yourself in the possibility mindset so that you build a muscle of being proactive rather than reactive when it comes to being faced with problems.

2. **Think of reasons why you can do something rather than on why you can't.** Anyone can come up with lots of reasons why something won't work. Only a few people can come up with lots of reasons why something can work, or will work. Become one of those people. Be the one to hear a co-worker's insane idea or dream and say, "I think you can do that!" or "That's totally possible," and then work to help him/her come up with reasons why it will work.

3. **Start.** Contrary to popular belief, you don't need to "believe to achieve." You just need to get started and take action, one step at a time. I did not believe in myself when I started school in Romania because I had never done these things (math, physics,

chemistry) before. But, I knew that if I continued to move forward, taking action, those things would change.

4. **Set high goals**. There is a saying that goes, "If you aim for the stars, even if you fall short, you can still land on the moon."

5. **Understand the difference between your destination goal and your performance goals.** Determine what you need to learn to reach your destination. I wanted to be a successful man, but I had to understand that along the way, my performance goals (meaning learning the skills I needed to become successful) were just as important as my destination.

THE RESILIENCE MINDSET

"Our greatest glory is not in never falling, but in rising every time we fall."
—Confucius

Just as you can't learn patience without being put into situations that demand it, you can't learn resilience unless you encounter and deal with disappointment, loss, or hardship. I was about to encounter the most opportune change for my personal development, even though it would be the most difficult change for my personal life. Romania, as difficult and challenging as it was, would be a gift because it taught me the resilience mindset.

When I left Canada, I had not, unfortunately, graduated from high school. While living there, I had made a lot of good friends and had also progressed greatly in my learning. As I also shared earlier, Canada had afforded me the ability to enjoy the best time in my life up to that point, in terms of my learning and development.

But, everything changed when my dad called me saying that he had received a fax from Liberia. He said, "We are going to be moving to Romania." It was a real shock to me. My wonderful life in high school was about to be turned upside down. Because I didn't see it coming, I was very poorly prepared to move to a new place, especially a communist country. It felt to me that we were expected to get packed, leave our life in Canada behind, and get to Romania as soon as we could.

By that time, I had been promoted to the eleventh grade. I was now twenty. I reminisced about my arrival in Canada three years before. I had been placed in the ninth grade based on my age, not my prior educational experience. I was so grateful I was able to spend almost three wonderful years in Canada before we left for Romania. Those three years helped prepare me for my next mindset lesson.

Our departure from Canada was not planned at all. For my dad, it was a promotion to the next level. I discovered that we had just a couple of months to prepare for the move. I hated to leave my school and the many good friendships I had formed. Actually, it was when I told my friends that I was going to be leaving, that they first realized I was not a Canadian and that my father was a diplomat. The Canadian culture is so permissive; they didn't care where I came from.

At the end of the school year, all my teachers wished me well as my last day at school approached, making it very touching. Besides the parties with my friends, I also frequently visited them at their homes, trying to enjoy their company for as much as I could before leaving. On behalf of my dad and me, the Embassy organized receptions to wish my dad farewell and success on his new assignment.

The morning of our departure, the Embassy chauffeur took us to the airport. We caught our flight which took an entire day. We had to change planes because it was not a direct flight. In those days, direct flights to Romania were few and far between. There were probably just three or four direct flights from Europe to Romania. Communism was in full swing there when we arrived.

When we finally got there, it was night. I was shocked because the airport was so dark, feeling quite surreal. There were armed officers everywhere. Because on our route we had changed planes in a modern European airport, I expected the Romanian airport to be at least similar to that airport. I never thought it could be so incredibly different. I realized that I really knew nothing about Romania. Seeing those armed guards all over the place and starting to experience what the country was all about was a major shock.

Upon our arrival, we were escorted to the airport's diplomatic waiting room. There was a VIP lounge where we waited for the staff from the Liberian Embassy. We didn't speak the language, and because it was our first time in Romania, our airport clearance process was taken over by the Embassy staff.

The only similarity to our departure from Canada was the diplomatic car waiting for us, along with a chauffeur from the Embassy. That was one of the few things that felt at least a little familiar. But, this ride was eerie and quite strange. I remember as we rode away from the airport that night, the streets were pitch black.

During those years in Romania, the streetlights were turned off at night. This was during the height of a Communist era, where the policy was basically scarcity of everything: electricity, gas, and even the lights on the street. Most of the houses were hidden by the darkness. A cold chill ran up my spine looking at those streets. My first impression of Romania was that it was pretty much the polar opposite of Ottawa, and that it felt intimidating and scary.

I stayed home for the first month, which was not all that bad. I was getting accustomed to the new environment and making new friends. My father was busy getting acclimated to the embassy and taking over the responsibilities from the current ambassador.

On our second day at the residence, the chauffeur introduced to us the lady who was going to take care of my dad and me. She was the maid. It turned out that the embassy staff had already hired her before we arrived. She became someone who, for many years, even after she was not working for us anymore and until she passed away, was a presence in my life and the life of my family. Her name was Mariana, and she was a wonderful person. Mariana was Romanian, but she had previously worked for different African embassies in Bucharest, so she knew how to cook our traditional menus, which was very important for our diet.

During those years, there were a lot of bilateral agreements between Romania and the African states, resulting in an impressive number of students coming from all over the African countries to complete their studies in Romania. I soon discovered that there were many African and Liberian students studying in Romania. Compared to the situation in Canada, where there had been no Liberian students, in Romania, many of them were studying topics in universities like medicine, pharmacy, and economics, and some were even pursuing their PhDs.

With so many Liberian and African students around, I began to feel more at home, and like I belonged to a community. At the same time, this brought to light one of my father's very important values: soon he became, in a sense, their surrogate father. Our home was always open to the Liberian students. Most of them came after their studies to have a decent meal. Mariana would cook enough food so that anytime we had a visitor, they would have something to eat.

For the Liberian community and even many other foreign students, our residence became their second home in many ways. This was all possible because of my father's openness to receive them at any time and to sort of cater to their needs.

As I got to know better the Liberian and African students who loved hanging around our home, I realized being part of that community created a sense of unity. I found this to be very supportive as I was learning to develop my resilience, which I needed in order to adapt and go on with my studies. It also helped me to learn the local culture as well as the local and national laws. Moreover, it was often a lot of fun! This was another blessing.

Most of the students were older than I, with a few of them around my age. In a way, some of them became my mentors. Having been in Romania for many years, they were quite knowledgeable about the local culture. They taught me how to get around in Bucharest, or how to handle local cultural issues that were not evident on the surface. There were many restrictions in terms of movement during those days. But, after living for some time in a country under a communist government, they were in a position to better explain to us what it meant to be foreigners here.

One of the privileges I enjoyed, being the son of a diplomat in Romania, was the access to special diplomatic stores that existed because of the absolute scarcity at that time. I took great pleasure going to the diplomatic stores with most of the students in order to shop for them, mainly for groceries and basic needs that were not available in the local stores because of the food shortages in the country.

Upon our arrival in Romania, our family started growing when my dad married Willia Eugenia Trinity. Shortly afterwards, a new member of the family arrived, when my stepmother gave birth to my beloved little sister Eugenia Jane-Ann. We all called her EJ. I now had a new stepmother and a little sister to look after and inspire.

Later on, the family would increase again, this time due to the ongoing civil war back in Liberia. One of the Liberian students studying in Romania had to leave as his specialization was completed. This student had a child named Billy with a Romanian girl. He had taken Billy in his care at the residence while awaiting his allowance and air ticket from Liberia. Unfortunately, he didn't receive sufficient funds, just one air ticket; therefore, he was forced to leave Billy, at the age of three, in the care of my father.

New Challenges and More Challenges

Back in Canada, I had become settled in terms of making progress in my education. But, since we left Canada before I finished high school, I had to complete grades 11 and 12 in Romania, no less! Moreover, moving to Romania meant that I now had to study in a foreign language.

Remember, I only started to read and write properly at the age of 15. For that reason, in terms of languages, mastering the English language was my sole motivation, focus and goal. In Canada, I also had the option to study French as a second language, but being a foreign student, I was not obliged to study it. Therefore, I skipped all the classes, concentrating on English only.

After only three years of schooling in Canada, I came to Romania, where there were no options of studying in my language. Romanian was the only language of study in all the public schools here. In order to not get discouraged, I would have to learn and adopt a different mindset.

Being diplomats, it took time for my documents to be processed and for me to get approval to start school. Not only that, but as a diplomat's son, I couldn't attend just any school. In fact, I had to get special approval from the Romanian government to attend school at all. So, all of that red tape slowed down my admittance to school.

When all of my paperwork was finally completed, I started school in Bucharest in the eleventh grade at the age of 20. It was really late as the school year had only a few months left. Besides that, trying to gain at least a rudimentary grasp of the language proved to be almost impossible during the time I was waiting for my paperwork to be approved.

Normally at that age, in Romania as well as in many parts of the world, children are already ahead in their university or college studies. But, I knew that I had to go the extra mile, working harder than ever before in order to graduate from high school.

I had to adapt to the multiple changes and challenges I was thrown into. The Canadian culture and school system were totally different. I found myself transplanted in this new, strange country that was essentially the antithesis of my life in Canada. I had no more control, and far less freedom of choice. In Canada, following my assessment evaluation, I had been attending a high school with an economics and business profile, but no advanced level mathematics, physics or chemistry. In Romania, however, in the 11th grade, college level mathematics and sciences were part of the compulsory subjects of study.

The study of Romanian literature was also required. It was a huge challenge for me, but one that I knew I had to overcome if I were to succeed in graduating from high school. This is when I gradually discovered what the resilience mindset must be. Because I was faced with so many challenges, I had to become resilient in order to survive in school and succeed. Learning the Romanian language, and simultaneously learning algebra, physics, and chemistry felt absolutely overwhelming at times. There were so many hurdles to get past.

Compared to Canada, Romania was like night and day in just about every way, including culture and environment. This was a communist country, and I had to be strong, resilient, and adapt quickly. Otherwise, I wouldn't have stood a chance of completing my education. I had already discovered other important mindsets, but this time around, I became conscious that I needed to get through a much tougher version of high school. This clearly showed me there were many difficulties and setbacks as a result of my not having completed high school in Canada.

But through it all, I always remembered what my birth mom told me and implanted in my subconscious: I was going to become a big man. In my mind, the only way that I could see ever become a successful man was to overcome the new challenges that I faced. I was conscious of what I had to do. I had to accept those changes and challenges in order to succeed. I had just learned how to read and write in English, and now, I needed to learn at another level in a completely foreign language.

Fifth "Curve"

As I shared earlier, the public school system in Romania was like night and day in comparison to Canada's. Normally, I would have needed to learn the Romanian language before starting school, but I didn't have time. School had already begun, and the diplomatic red tape took a few months while processing my school documents. So, I started school with just a very basic knowledge of the Romanian language.

I was also learning the language at home, after school and on weekends. Once again, I had to catch up, which was proving to be a recurring theme in the story of my life. Besides learning a new language, I discovered my ability to retain visual information and reproduce it. I had to memorize lots of information and formulas that I didn't understand at all. But, this ability was a requirement in order for me to get through high school. It was my only chance.

Luckily, I made friends pretty quickly and easily. I was able to acquire the basic courses from my friends, especially a girlfriend of mine, Simona, who helped me a great deal. She took notes for me and helped me grasp a bit of everything from the ocean of information given to me. I would come home and read the notes or textbooks many times, basically memorizing all of the important parts and formulas so that I could pass my tests. I was reading the information over and over and over.

Before each test, I would wake up at 5:00 a.m. and double-check myself to see if I still remembered the theory and formulas. I had not been exposed to anything similar in my previous education, and it was very stressful.

I acknowledged new faculties that I wasn't aware I had and put them to work. I discovered and embraced a new powerful resilience mindset that I absolutely needed if I was to succeed. All of these played a huge role in my getting through those last years of high school. Finally, graduating from high school at the age of 22 was a huge achievement for me. If I look back now at how, where and when I started and then comprehend my learning curve, I can say it again, graduation was a huge achievement for me. I cleared my first hurdle to becoming a "big man."

1989 Romanian Revolution

A year after our arrival in Romania in 1989, I witnessed the fall of President Nicolae Ceausescu, considered one of the most brutal dictators of the Eastern European Communist bloc.

The revolution started on December 16 in the city of Timisoara, located in the Western part of Romania. After several days of protesting, the army and security forces cracked down on the protesters who were demonstrating against the Communist regime policies. This left many protesters seriously injured and some dead. The news quickly reached other cities across the country, including Bucharest.

On the morning of December 21, hundreds of people (many brought by the Communist party in buses) gathered in front of President Ceausescu's Palace to see him deliver his speech condemning the uprising in Timisoara. Some of the people in the crowd began booing him and shouting "Timisoara" immediately after he started his speech. Within a few hours, the incident quickly turned into widespread protest against Ceausescu and his regime. This marked the fall of Communism in Romania.

For some reason, my dad didn't go to work on that day. As the second part of the day approached, we heard gunshots. The protest had gained ground during the day and involved the police, the Securitate. This was the professional state security force, and the army against the civilians seemed to be the only solution for President Ceausescu to crack down on the protest.

Our residence was located about 1.5 miles from the Revolution Square. My dad tried to reach his staff and students to see if they were all right, but he couldn't. There was little he could do because the phone lines were down, and we had no access to any source of communication. We couldn't leave the residence. It wasn't safe for us or for any foreigners during those days of the uprising and the crackdown. I remembered seeing my dad glued to his radios all day, listening to the BBC News, and

Voice of America. They were the only sources of information we had that were in English.

University

After high school graduation, it was time for me to choose my university studies. I enrolled in one of the best universities in Romania, the Bucharest University of Economic Studies. However, I ended up again missing the start of my university classes because I was waiting on my scholarship funding—more diplomatic red tape.

When I started university, I had already missed the first few weeks of the courses. Again, this was a setback from which I thought I could hardly recover. One major shock for me was that the very first course I attended was Technology. This subject dealt with refineries and anything else that you might imagine that you probably would never need in life. I sat there stunned as our professor spoke for 45 minutes nonstop. To make matters worse, I understood nothing about those huge diagrams she was drawing on the blackboard.

Thankfully, my ability to make friends quickly came in handy. After the first course, I met some new colleagues, and one of the first things I inquired about was who they thought was a serious student who could lend me course notes. There was this quiet, serious girl sitting in the first row who didn't interact much with anybody. Her name was Brindusa. That girl just happens to be my wife today.

After the collapse of the communist government in Romania, things in everyday life were changing rapidly. Romania was on a fast track towards a market economy and new opportunities were arising everywhere. Also, my Romanian had gotten much better. I was almost fluent, but starting in the second year at university, I was thankfully able to study in English once more. By that time, they had set up different sections of the university where you could study in the French or English language. I was transferred to the English section, where my life became so much easier. Finally, something familiar! I was very happy and relieved to be studying in English once again.

The Resilient Mind

Ford Did Have a Better Idea

Ford Motor Company adopted the slogan, "Ford Has a Better Idea" in 2012, and they had the track record to prove it. You always have the opportunity to learn from industry leaders who have fought through a comeback, either due to an economic crisis or because of poor business decisions, such as the case of the collapse of the US auto industry in 2008.

Alan Mulally became CEO of Ford Motor Company in the fall of 2006. At that time, the company was on the precipice of bankruptcy. It was in severe debt, and that was the most abysmal year in its history, having suffered over $12 billion in losses. When Mulally retired in 2014, Ford had done what many deemed impossible and made a massive turnaround. What was it about his leadership and use of the resilience mindset that brought this about?

His own words hold some of the answers: "Leadership is having a compelling vision, a comprehensive plan, relentless implementation, and talented people working together. People also want meaning. All of us want to know that we are doing great things, that we are touching a lot of people, and that what we are doing is something bigger than ourselves."

After holding the CEO post a mere three months, Mulally made an unheard of pitch to the largest US banks at a conference in New York. He offered to mortgage the entirety of Ford's assets in exchange for loans to renovate the company and get it back on its feet. Even though that approach was largely viewed as a desperate act, because Mulally was thinking outside the box and making use of his resilience mindset, he was able to convince the banks to give Ford $23.6 billion in loans.

Putting those funds to brilliant use under his leadership, Ford had one of the biggest bounce-back victories in business history. Mulally spearheaded a partnership agreement with the United Auto Workers, who signed on to create a number of shifts to improve the company's profit margins in a tradeoff where Ford guaranteed the return of production jobs to the US.

He was also successful in consolidating the company's purchases from vendors who agreed to become Ford's partners. This enabled them to lower costs in Ford's favor and brought them a larger portion of the business.

When GM and Chrysler hit extremely hard times in the three years following Ford's securing of the bank loans, they appealed to the federal government for help. Although Mulally didn't need that assistance, he testified on behalf of his competitors, and thereby, contributed to the decision of the government to create the Auto Industry Bailout in 2009.

Mulally knew that if his two rivals, General Motors and Chrysler, went under, it would damage the suppliers' network, the auto industry overall and Ford itself. He felt that advocating on their behalf was just "the right thing to do." His leadership was cutting edge when it came to both thinking outside of the box and applying a resilience mindset. It is a stellar example of successful reinvention based upon those very principles.

Sports Legends Demonstrate Resilience

We can also learn from sport legends who went through difficult periods during their careers, yet still made great comebacks. Legends like Tiger Woods, Roger Federer and Rafael Nadal have all proven themselves to be remarkably resilient. Tiger Woods's comeback in September 2018 absolutely took the golfing world by surprise.

Learning from others is always preferable to reinventing the wheel and learning through your own challenges. Both are excellent teachers, but when we learn from others, we save time, effort, and disappointment. Don't worry. You will always have your own personal challenges that will teach you things, but when you can read about, or watch a video of what others have overcome, and how they did it, watch, listen, and learn.

Resilience Mindset Properties

The resilience mindset in your toolkit of life skills is invaluable. It enables you to bounce back from seemingly insurmountable odds and challenges. This mindset can also guide you through those times when life throws you a curve. Rather than succumbing and giving up when faced with rejection, fear, worry, and loss, employing the resilience mindset makes it much easier to focus on solutions. It will also help keep you from feeling overwhelmed by problems. Instead, it will put you in the driver's seat to implement change and discover solutions.

Resilience is an innate quality that we all possess. It's simply a matter of choosing to employ it when discouragement crops up, instead of throwing in the towel and giving up. Adopting a resilience mindset will deepen and broaden your other skillsets. It will enable you to handle challenges with a greater sense of control. This sense of control then stays with you and impacts your life in ways that will empower you. You will then mitigate the risk of events snowballing into other areas of your life.

Now at age 50, I realize that my educational path was far from easy. It was no walk in the park, as the saying goes. It has always been a difficult climb for me in many ways, but still I have always been driven to aim high. Unfortunately, I skipped early childhood education and slipped past several years of elementary and secondary education, but I still made it to one of the most prestigious universities available to me, the Bucharest University of Economic Studies. I graduated with an MBA.

I have been fortunate to work in multinational companies like Vodafone (formerly Connex) as channel project manager. I oversaw the marketing activities of more than 500 business dealers across Romania when I worked at Vodafone. I also worked for Exact Software Romania, a Dutch software company that offers accounting, Enterprise Resource Planning and other software for small and medium enterprises.

At Exact Software, I worked as a sales manager and was responsible for developing the market in Romania. Over the last 19 years, I set up my own business and have provided thousands of full-time jobs and tens of thousands of part-time jobs to students across Romania. Coming from such humble beginnings, I have tears in my eyes now as I recall my strange and wonderful journey,

If it weren't for the resilience mindset, I don't know how I would have kept going during all of my challenges. I had no idea during my school years that my future in this gray, difficult environment actually would be the base that led me to a very powerful and rewarding path, one that I still follow today.

Steps to Integrate the Resilience Mindset into Your Daily Life

Resilience is the capacity or ability to recover quickly from difficulties. It is mental, emotional, and physical toughness. Resilient people always bounce back and never give up, no matter what life throws at them. It's a skill you develop over time, and a skill you can't develop unless you encounter many trying and frustrating situations in your life. It's like weight lifting; you can't develop big muscles unless you lift big weights. The more adversity you overcome, the more resilient you become.

1. **Increase your sense of control in areas where you have control.** This could be in simple ways such as arriving on time, eating healthfully, employing good sleeping habits, and scheduling enjoyable types of exercise.

2. **Observe resilient people.** Use them as role models. Human beings learn largely by observation. Frequent venues where you can watch people exhibiting the skills you wish to acquire. Read books about people who have overcome obstacles similar to those you face. Call or write them. Ask them to share their lessons learned. Their success will be contagious.

3. **Maintain your perspective around challenges.** Resist the urge to see any event as insurmountable. This can be cultivated by applying that perspective to small difficulties throughout the day.

4. **Develop your resilience muscles.** This can be accomplished in many small ways throughout your day. Notice and observe your adaptive abilities, and feel appreciation for those skills. Shift to a positive mindset when you feel doubt or reservation. Taking this approach will enable the growth of

those skills, which once seen, can be intensified.

5. **Challenge yourself to get out of your comfort zone by accepting new provocations from others.** Don't be afraid; we are all born with infinite potential. You just need to believe in yourself and allow time to develop your craft.

6. **Create your New Year's resolutions and respect them.** It's about training your mind to keep focus. Keeping focus builds resilience and positive thinking.

7. **Take on an assignment that will open up your thinking even if it initially scares you.** Resilience is about thinking beyond where others have limitations. It has positive effects on the brain and energizes the body to move forward when thinking of the positive outcome.

8. **Don't be afraid to take on another assignment even if you failed the first one.** Remember, failure doesn't measure your abilities or potential for future success. You just need to work harder to develop the abilities needed to overcome those challenges.

9. **Consider developing a faith habit.** Those who have a faith practice have been shown to have more resilience in crisis. Hope is a powerful motivator and belief in a higher power creates the ability to sustain us through demanding times.

10. **Practice mindfulness through meditation.** Meditation has been well researched, and is found to benefit our well-being in a variety of ways. Meditation changes the structure of the brain, thereby creating a greater sense of overall peace and well-being.

Research has uncovered the following benefits of meditation:

- Greater emotional regulation
- Improves insight and the ability to employ broader perspective
- Decreases stress
- Lowers anxiety and depression
- Improves memory and focus
- Reduces high blood pressure

I know that many people find meditation hard and often impossible. My suggestion is to start with just five minutes each morning by quieting your mind. Then focus on your breathing. This short break can make a big difference from what is often going on in our brains, referred to as the "monkey mind." That's when ideas flash in and out all day long, and for many, can keep them up at night.

How can you increase your awareness and ability? Practice the skill of staying in the moment. Develop this discipline by stopping yourself from reviewing past concerns and future fears. The book *The Power of Now* by Eckhart Tolle is an excellent guide for this practice.

THE PASSION MINDSET

One interpretation of the word "passion" means to do something that you like doing without a paycheck attached. To develop the passion mindset you must totally love what you are doing. If you don't, then you must find that thing that stirs this mindset within you.

As Steve Jobs said so eloquently, "You've got to find what you love. And that is as true for your work as it is for your lovers. Your work is going to fill a large part of your life, and the only way to be truly satisfied is to do what you believe is great work. And the only way to do great work is to love what you do. If you haven't found it yet, keep looking. Don't settle. As with all matters of the heart, you'll know when you find it. And, like any great relationship, it just gets better and better as the years roll on. So keep looking until you find it. Don't settle."[5]

---

[5] https://www.forbes.com/sites/timworstall/2011/10/08/steve-jobs-and-the-dont-settle-speech/#76e2fd2e7437

Work

While still a student in Bucharest, it seemed to me that during the time I'd been living in Romania I had faced many unexpected challenges. As it turned out, the first job that I got there was filled with opportunities to challenge myself.

I was in the fourth year of my studies when I got my first job. During that summer, besides feeling a bit bored, I craved new, enriching experiences. Getting a job seemed the perfect way to move forward. However, I had the handicap of not speaking perfect Romanian. I had to rely on English, although I was still far from mastering it on any advanced level. Still, my only option was a job where my English skills could be of use. I was lucky that a friend of mine heard about a vacant editor position at a newspaper published in English in Bucharest.

In Romania in the early 1990s, there were very few English-language magazines. This daily newspaper happened to be one of the leading publications to appear solely in that language. In fact, it was dedicated to the diplomatic and expat community. The newspaper was distributed in all the major hotels in Romania.

I applied for the position, summoned up my courage, went for the interview, and got the job. What the owners of the newspaper had in mind when they hired me as an editor was that I could use some translation skills to check the accuracy of the translation from Romanian to English. The fact that I was a native English speaker who knew sufficient Romanian to understand the original written articles seemed to fit the bill. I had to make sure that the stories translated to English were actually what the journalists wanted to communicate.

This required meeting with the journalists and listening to their stories and what they had in mind when writing them. Next, I had to proofread the articles to ensure that the English content was in alignment with the original Romanian storyline. Of course, I was well aware that I wasn't entirely ready for the responsibilities of that job, but I knew I could compensate through hard work. I was prepared to put in any extra time needed in order to deliver the quality of writing that the job required.

I was in charge of reading all the articles in English with an editorial eye. This meant making sure to eliminate grammatical errors, correcting misspellings, and rephrasing sentences as needed.

Boy, it was a challenge! I went in early and was among the last to leave when the newspaper was ready to go to the printing house. Sometimes, I had to stop the paper from being printed because at the last minute I discovered that something wasn't right, and I had to correct it.

I remember telling my dad about my new job. I wasn't expecting this from him, but he was so proud of me! Because truthfully, during those days, diplomats did not work. Period. Being the son of a diplomat in Romania was something that most kids would have relished. You didn't have to work. You had everything at your disposal. But for me, that was not ideal.

Being the son of a diplomat was certainly something I was proud of. That my humble beginnings in a tiny village had culminated in the opportunities I was now being afforded - all of this was amazing, don't get me wrong. But, it was not enough for me. I felt something was missing, and that is why I applied for this job.

What was important for me was the fact that I was able to go out there, get a job by myself without the help of my dad, and at the same time, I was able to expose myself to the real world. This is what I had been waiting for and what all my schooling had prepared me for. This job was even more significant for me because working at the newspaper with the title of "editor" was a big deal in those days, and I loved to impress!

Because I was in my fourth year at the university, I knew I needed to prove to myself that I was ready for the outside world. This was crucial. During those months of being an editor, I acquired self-confidence and self-sufficiency. At the end of the summer, the newspaper's manager offered to allow me to continue working, even during the remainder of my studies. I could resume my classes, and after they ended for the day, I could work at the newspaper. It was a good arrangement.

Most of the articles came in toward the second part of the day. In the mornings, the journalists went out to interview people, or would go to different events where they collected their stories. Then, when they came back to the newspaper office, they would start writing their articles. Their schedule accommodated me attending classes, and afterwards being able to continue my job. So, in a way, it felt like it was meant to be. I continued to work with the newspaper for another month. By that time, the paper had hired a second editor, allowing me to leave without creating an interruption to the business. I will always be grateful for that first job opportunity.

My first job ingrained in me the values of hard work and responsibility. Yes, I worked far more hours than I was paid for, but that was all right. The aim was for me to deliver an excellent product I could be proud of. The fact that my dad would be reading the product of my work every day put extra pressure on me, so I loved doing it even more. That first job was extremely important to me. I took pride in working hard to get the best results possible.

The passion was there. It was reflected in my dedication and willingness to work harder because of how much I still had to learn. Striving first to deliver high quality work rather than solely working with financial compensation in mind was due to my passion. I define the word *passion* to mean doing something that you love without needing a paycheck.

It's a belief, a credo, a hope, a dream. It's that thing that transforms into reality through hard work, dedication, and continuous commitment. That's when it delivers the real benefits and results.

Passion is like the fluid of blood in your veins - it keeps you alive. You might say it's the lifeblood of your soul. It keeps you awake at night. It makes you shine when performing a task. As long as you have passion, it will benefit you to strive for your best no matter the challenges. It will give you strength to move forward.

In order to transform passion into results and real benefits, you must do as Dr. Martin Luther King Jr. suggested: "He should sweep streets so well that all the hosts of heaven and earth will pause to say, 'Here lived a great street sweeper who did his job well.'"

My next job was in sales. Sweeping the hallways of heaven was what my love and passion for a sales job felt like to me. The more meetings I got, the more sales I locked down, and the more I was able to shine in the hallways of heaven so that the angels could notice me.

I still had difficulties speaking the local language, but due to my passion, I didn't see that as a setback. Many of my clients appreciated my efforts, which sometimes helped in closing the deal.

My entire life has been filled with passion. Even the little things that I do are full of life. I put a lot of energy into what I do. It doesn't matter whether I'm going to succeed or fail. The effort I expend is part of my passion. The energy that I put into things that I do - like my first job - for me, that was a sign of passion. If I had treated this job like most kids look at summer jobs, just doing it for the money, I don't think that I would have been able to keep the job. And, I certainly would not have been offered the possibility to continue during my final year at the university.

Ever since I was a child in Liberia, my passion in life has been to deliver results. Whatever I do, wherever I go, I want to deliver positive results. I want to make a positive impact on whomever I meet. That's my passion in life.

Learning. Learning before all. I have a passion for lifelong learning. *No matter what, even if I fail, I know I'm going to learn and grow.* Here are three questions to ask yourself to grow your passion mindset:

1. What is the common thing that your family and friends have said is most special about you? For example, are you known as the life of the party, or the best cook?

2. What is something you love doing so much that you lose track of time when engaged in it?

3. Who is one of your role models? What one attribute do they possess that you love the most? Note that this trait is most likely related to a passion of yours.

Passion for Innovation

You can have more than one passion. In fact, it's good to have several passions, as they will support and enrich each other. One of my passions today as a businessperson is around innovation. My passion to be innovative has actually caused me to set up some high standards for myself, but in the end, it has been all worthwhile.

For example, I strived to create a leading agency in the Romanian market. By setting this goal, I put into action a set of steps to achieve it, such as innovating different types of services within our target markets. My strategy paid off, leading to a joint venture with a US-based company. I brought them into Romania, offering services to the market that did not exist at that time. I also brought many new business ideas to

Romania that were not yet available in the market. Some of them were successful, and some weren't.

I love to discover new ideas. My love for creativity must have been seeded in me during my childhood. In my village, we didn't have toys. We also didn't have money. We didn't have any stores in our village. In fact, we used to build our own cars. In order for you to have a toy, you needed to build one. So, we found pieces of wood and designed our own cars. Using empty food cans of tuna, coupled with the magic of our imagination and innovation - voila! We transformed those into a beautiful car!

Children are so good at pretending and seeing things through their imagination. I believe many of the most successful adults on the planet have learned to befriend their inner child to open up their hearts and minds to rich possibilities. Passion becomes the spark that ignites innovation and imagination, enabling you to see far beyond what's right in front of you at the drawing board. This is where your passion mindset can leverage opportunity for greatness in your life.

Famous People Who Employed the Passion Mindset

Walt Disney

Walt Disney had a passion mindset about drawing and cartooning from the time he was a young boy. Around the age of nine or ten, he was selling his paintings and drawings to family, friends, and neighbors. In high school, he took classes in photography and art, and created cartoons for his school paper. In the evenings, he continued focusing on his passion, studying at the Art Institute of Chicago. When he was 18, he moved to Kansas City to take a job his brother Roy got for him at a professional art studio.

He worked for a time at a newspaper, but was fired for having a "lack of imagination and good ideas," which seems inconceivable now. Yet, even when others doubted his talent and abilities, he forged onward, driven by his passion for art.

About that time, he started exploring, using a camera with his art, experimenting with hand-drawn cells to be used in animation. Shortly thereafter, he started his own animation company, which produced a number of cartoons, including seven-minute fairy tales. During the 1920s, his studio went bankrupt. Undeterred, Walt and Roy decided to move to Hollywood and started their own company, Disney Brothers' Studio.

Disney cartoons grew in scope and were expanded with an array of characters he created. These have become household names such as Mickey Mouse, Donald Duck, Pluto, Goofy, and more. His cartoon titled *Flowers and Trees* was the first ever to be made in color, and it went on to win an Oscar.

Disney had a number of setbacks throughout his life, including the theft of one of his early characters, Oswald the Lucky Rabbit. But, he always found ways to bounce back and stay focused on his life's passion: animation. His cartoons went on to win a total of 22 Academy Awards, and he and Roy founded Disneyland and Disney World. He truly exemplifies the heights a career fueled by the passion mindset is capable of achieving.

J. K. Rowling

The creator of Harry Potter's rags to riches story is fairly well-known, but it bears repeating here, that her passion mindset is what led her to massive success.

A young single mom for a time, Rowling worked as a researcher and secretary. Rowling has said she was inspired to create Harry Potter while riding on a train to work. During the next seven years, she went through many hardships, including the death of her mother, divorce, losing her job, and as a result, having to deal with poverty. Still, her passion mindset kept her writing, and her first book *Harry Potter and the Philosopher's Stone* was published in 1997.

Knowing that the target market for the books was young boys, she decided to use her initials, J. K., to remove any prejudice about a woman author creating tales of a boy wizard. Little did she know that her books and the resulting films would become a big hit with millions of adults as well.

She went on to become the first billionaire author. She lost that status intentionally by donating a large portion of her wealth to charitable causes. She still is the bestselling living author in the UK, and has proven herself to be seemingly endless in her creativity and humanitarianism.

Rowling's passion mindset is living proof that if you don't lose sight of your dreams no matter what hand life deals you, but work hard and persist, success may welcome you with open arms.

Vulnerability

The passion mindset also involves staying vulnerable. Me? I'm still vulnerable. It's actually very useful in an online world that is centered in authenticity and transparency. You cannot achieve success there without a level of vulnerability. It can also help you *stay ready* to leverage the areas of your life that need tending to, areas where you can ask for help.

Asking for help, one way of being vulnerable, led me to my writing coach. She has helped me improve my writing skills by challenging me to reach deeply within, encouraging me every step of the way. Without her enthusiasm, support, and guidance, I don't know whether I could have completed this book. I love that parts of it may help others address their own vulnerabilities. I thank her for that.

It's true that I still have weak spots, places where I'm vulnerable. But, I also know our vulnerability only makes us more real, authentic, and relatable. Ultimately, as long as we acknowledge our soft spots and address them, these vulnerabilities turn into strengths. With constant attention and acceptance of our vulnerable spots, we break through to a stronger self.

In my last year of university studies, I began working as a sales agent at a telecommunication company. I use the word "telecom" company, but actually, it was a paging company. Paging is now outdated, even antiquated. But, it's important to note that paging was the beginning of texting and consisted of very short messages. Many times it just displayed a phone number to call back. But still, this was the genesis of texting. When I began working there, I was 27 years old.

My girlfriend Brindusa (now my wife) got a job at the paging company before I did. I was surprised how easily she got that job because she was shy and not a salesperson type. But for me, getting a position as a sales agent in such a place as the paging company would have meant so much. It's difficult to comprehend now just how important getting that position would have meant to me. This was all related to my childhood impression about what my stepfather back in Liberia, starting as a sales agent, had achieved.

The company was called Bel Pagette Romania. It was owned by a Serbian-Canadian businessman named Zoran. It was one of the top paging companies during the mid-1990s in Romania.

I applied for the job and to my sheer joy, got it. As sales agents, our pay was strictly commission based, no salary. There was a one-day training and off we went, looking for customers on the market. I was assigned to a team leader that would supervise our day-to-day activities. Brindusa was also working under his supervision, so we quickly formed a team. I was responsible for setting up the meetings, making the presentations and negotiating, while she handled calculations and contracts. Fortunately, we both excelled in our areas of responsibility. Therefore, we made a great team.

Being new to the business, I sat in the office the first several days, observing how my colleagues were working. On the wall there was a list of general managers at certain companies considered unapproachable. But those were the biggest companies in Romania, and therefore, had the highest potential to buy pagers.

Inquiring why my colleagues couldn't contact these companies, I discovered the problem was that they couldn't get past the secretaries. The phone calls would not be transferred to the managers, the decision makers.

My strategy was to get to the office before 7:30 in the morning, a time when I knew that the secretaries weren't going to be on duty, yet. Therefore, that's when I started to make my sales calls. During those days, there were only landlines. The mobile telephone was not yet available. When I dialed the number, guess who answered the phone? The general manager/CEO. Why? Most of the major companies during those days were managed by expats. Expats went to work early in the morning.

I think I realized that because of my dad. Although he was an ambassador, he used to leave the house very early to go to the office, earlier than the rest of the staff. Assuming that could be a trait shared by other CEOs, I expected to find them alone in their offices early in the mornings, long before their secretaries arrived for work. It turned out my hunch was right!

Once I had unlocked that secret, it became my routine to go to the office early, make my calls, and then set appointments with those companies, previously considered untouchable. When I arrived at Bel Pagette, the highest number of pagers ever sold on a contract was somewhere around 10. The commission system was beyond generous for that amount. But, when you sold more than 10 pagers, the reward was more like heaven on earth.

My first contract, together with Brindusa, proved to be an astonishing feat! Do you want to venture a guess of how many pagers we sold with a one-year subscription? Sixty-six pagers! The commission we received from that first sale crippled the company that month. It was outrageous; but for us, truly amazing. The company changed the commission system immediately after that. With that opportunity, I proved that with passion and innovation one can work wonders. I was thinking outside the box, and it worked.

Upon my graduation from university, I was promoted to sales manager. Soon after, I went on to become sales and marketing manager at Bel Pagette. That was the beginning of my career in Romania. The company's philosophy was centered on the passion concept created by Zoran. I was most definitely full of passion.

Zoran is also one of the best salespeople I've ever come across in my entire life. At Bel Pagette, passion meant how the people, attitude, service, sales, and innovation created an outstanding culture. This was the essence of their philosophy, and it was tied to my own beliefs about passion and success.

Every step of my life, every aim, every accomplishment, my sense of purpose - all of these are deeply connected with my roots, the beginning of my ride. Remember, my first stepfather back in Liberia embodied my idea of becoming a salesman first. It was the first rung on a ladder toward reaching success as a businessman. That's why following in his footsteps was part of my dream. I followed that dream with dedication, commitment, and passion, and therefore, delivered excellent results.

Also, starting my career at Bel Pagette kept me on the path of remaining in Romania. Because of my successful experience at Bel Pagette, I would go on to work for other top companies like Vodafone Romania and Exact Software Romania, and, ultimately, would set up my own business.

What I learned by applying the passion mindset to my work life was that it served as a constant springboard for opportunity. Why? People could see my passion, which translated to them as a spirit of commitment, coupled with a can-do attitude.

I'm sure you have seen the powerful difference you feel, for example, when you hear someone who exudes passion when singing or acting. You get engaged. You want to cheer them on.

Take a moment to think about the top three things you currently are most passionate about. Then, go to three people you know well and ask them what they think your top three passions are. See if they match what you think. Often they will share insights that surprise you. You see, we often don't realize that we might not be tapping into our passions to leverage our lives.

So, I encourage you to go once through this exercise of interviewing your friends and family. Then, on a daily basis, write more about your passion. Follow the steps below to grow your passion mindset.

Steps to Integrate the Passion Mindset into Your Daily Life

Many people do not know what they are passionate about. The first step to creating a passion mindset is acknowledging what you love. The second step is pursuing it.

1. **Ask yourself regularly, "What am I most passionate about?"** I've been asked so many times by friends and others what keeps me connected to my business, or why I'm so passionate about my business. So, here's my question to you: what are you most passionate about?

Look at those achievements in your life where financial drive wasn't your main motivator - you just wanted to do your part. If you were onstage at the National Opera, or playing tennis on center court at the US Open, you were where you wanted to be, fully engaged in your passion. For me, one of my main passions is running my advertising agency. Part of what drives that passion is that I see this as all about providing the best services possible to my clients.

Reflect on what you love doing so much that it doesn't necessarily matter if there is a financial benefit. Picture the final moments when you finished something you loved doing - the feeling of self-accomplishment, your smile - it's a sign of your passion mindset.

2. **Choose one or two passions that you can go back to when faced with other challenges in your life.** It could be building Legos, doing crossword puzzles,

biking cross-country, cooking, painting, playing tennis, going to the gym, and so on. Doing activities that you love brings back your confidence and relaxes your mind.

3. **Get coaching.** If you don't know what brings you passion, the solution is simple. Seek coaching to discover what your passion is. There are life coaches, mentors, even family members, and friends who can help you discover your passions.

1. My family home where I lived until the age of 10, before moving to live with my step parents in Monrovia.

2. The road to my village.

It was no easy walk. In the early hours of the morning, This was also the road that I would take with my mother and father to the next village. There I would meet with my uncle who would then take me to Monrovia to live with my first step parents.

3. Receiving advice from my mother – repeating those powerful words that I grabbed onto and did not let go of, "You will become a big man." This was, sadly, the last time when I saw her alive.

4. My father and mom in front of their new home they built in the village where I grew up.

5. My role model, mentor and beloved mother
   – Miatta Kamara

6. With my big brother Mustapha and my mother in Monrovia

7. My beloved stepfather – G. Marcus Kelley

8. With my stepfather in New York

9. Our home in Ottawa – party time with my MJ white socks ☺

10. The beginning of my Entrepreneurial Journey, with my partner Mihaela to my left and the A-team at that time ☺

11. New Year's celebration with my wife Brindusa and our two boys – Philip and Patrick.

12. Christmas time with the family. Let's party!

Passion for sports runs in the family:

13. Philip at age 5 with his role model, French tennis player Gael Monfils – former ATP world number 6 during a tournament in Bucharest.

14. He's a future champion - after I barely survived playing tennis with him ☺

15. Patrick with Carol Eduard Novak, Romanian Cycling Paralympic champion, and President of the Romanian Cycling Federation.

16. With Patrick at a mountain bike competition in Bulgaria.

   I will definitely not repeat it again. He's too fast for me. Finishing time between us was almost an hour ☹

05 THE COURAGE MINDSET

"Success is not final, failure is not fatal: it is the courage to continue that counts."
—Winston Churchill

Churchill's quote eloquently shares insight that constitutes the most important mantra you can carry throughout your life. It's something that I know has had a major influence on my path to success. Even as a young child, courage was necessary for me to just get by on a daily basis.

As a little kid, I used to walk with my mom and my dad between villages. This was a long, grueling walk as there were many kilometers between one village and the next. And you had to constantly stay alert because there were hazards each step of the way. I think part of my natural bravery comes from the fact that I had the perfect environment to develop courage in my early childhood.

I grew up in a place where bravery and courage were part of daily life. Going into the woods to look for dry wood to make a fire, down the road to bring water from the creek, or staying out of the way of wild animals, or just walking to the farm required bravery and courage for both adults and children.

The fact that I was brought up with different families, and was there to serve those families, impacted me differently. It's not like I was a foster child where I was given all the same benefits as their birth children. Yes, I was treated humanely, but I had tasks to perform every day in exchange for the care I received. I had to wash dishes, iron clothes, and go on errands to purchase bread and to shop. That was part of my preparation to become brave, and to later overcome difficulties with the courage to move on.

Courage is not the absence of fear. It is the ability to do something that frightens you even if you are scared the entire time you are doing it! Up until this point it sounds like things were hard or difficult for me, but they were not insurmountable or frightening. Later on, in my professional life, I was faced with situations even more frightening that I believe anyone else may have given up entirely had they been faced with the same obstacles.

I lost everything when I went through bankruptcy. I had to borrow money from friends. I was sued. Friends and investors turned on me and filed false reports so that I wound up being investigated for fraud in Romania. Without a courage mindset, I would have given up and never survived. That's why I think this is one of the most helpful and powerful mindsets to develop.

I graduated from university at age 28. The Bel Pagette position as sales and marketing manager was the job I held until graduation. This was where I developed my drive for passion that still lives in me today.

As is typical in the world of fast-evolving technology, the Romanian telecom market changed dramatically when mobile phone service providers entered the market. Paging service companies lost most of their customers virtually overnight, leading Zoran to immediately sell Bel Pagette.

When the epidemic started, my team went out in search of new opportunities. My role at that moment was to support them. I supported them with advice on how to prepare their Curriculum Vitae and wrote them letters of recommendation. In the end, I also needed to move on.

That was when I applied to Vodafone, without even knowing if they had any job vacancies. I just submitted my CV and letter of intention to the Human Resources Department. I was called a few days later. I guess Vodafone already knew about me because they also hired most of my sales team from Bel Pagette. Perhaps, they read the many letters I wrote and signed as sales and marketing manager of Bel Pagette.

Still, this was not an immediate offer of employment. I had to jump through many hoops and go through several interviews. It was a long, arduous process. But, my gut feeling was that it would all be worth it. I think I had six interviews, starting with Human Resources. Next, I completed assessments in the areas of sales, marketing and advertising, and finally, I interviewed with Karla, the Vice-President of Sales and Marketing.

During that final interview, I told a joke by asking Karla if Vodafone wanted to hire me secretly as the new CEO because my first name was the same as their current CEO, Al. I joked that hiring me as the new CEO to replace him might make it easier for the staff to accept the change. As it turned out, all of those other departments I had interviewed with wanted me. Now, following my meeting with her, the Vice-President had the final decision.

I felt really good. This was a unique feeling, unlike anything I ever had before, just knowing that I did well in front of those other managers during the interviews. When Karla shared that information with me and offered me the job, I became even more confident. It was a major aha moment. I was ready to play my role at the next level.

I was placed in charge of the dealer's network. At that time, I was managing about 500 dealers in Romania. I supervised the dealer's network from the channel marketing point of view. This included overseeing how they communicated, what marketing activities the dealers implemented with the support of Vodafone, and how they developed. It was a good job, and a great company to be part of.

With Vodafone, I traveled across Romania, doing my job while having fun at the same time. But after a year, I decided to leave because I didn't see myself growing there. Don't get me wrong. When I arrived at Vodafone, it was a beautiful job.

I had good colleagues and actually enjoyed the work. But, I soon found myself stuck. I realized why I wasn't reaching my full potential. I was no longer in sales; yet, sales was my passion. Sales has always been my passion and my dream.

So, I decided to leave and to start up my own business. At that time, I remember my director telling me, "Al, if you decide to start up a business in the telecom area, Vodafone will support half of your investment." That was a phenomenal offer! So, my first idea was to set up stores around the country to become dealers for Vodafone. I actually got the okay in principle for their support, which could have been an amazing opportunity.

Although it was still my dream to have my own company, I soon got a job offer that I couldn't refuse. This came from a Dutch company, Exact Software Romania. They dangled a major carrot in front of me: to become their sales manager for Romania. It was sales, and since that was my first love and passion, I took the job. I then went for training in the Netherlands, and when I came back, formed my sales team and set sales targets.

This was exciting, but things got better. After a short period of being together with my team, we far exceeded the set targets. This was amazing and very gratifying. I got the highest appreciation from the regional Vice- President of Sales and Marketing from the company headquarters in Delft. This was when I realized that I could sell any business idea that I wanted. It added to my ability to believe in myself.

I worked at Exact for one year. But then, I had to leave to start my company because I discovered something else about my selling skills shortly after my arrival: I could sell high-value services and products as easily as I sold inexpensive products. Enterprise Resource Planning software, consultancy, and implementation services were very expensive during the early years.

I had no savings to speak of. But, at that time, I was very close to going out on my own. I probably had about two paychecks saved up from Exact. So, I basically started my first company without any capital, without even thinking about what was awaiting me. I was in Romania, a foreign country. It was the year 2000 when I founded my company. This was 11 years after communism had collapsed. Romania was at the beginning of its economic development and was becoming an emerging market.

At the time I started my own company, my only true asset was my belief that I was going to succeed, no matter what I was going to do. I believed in myself so much that I made the decision to quit my job. I devoted my time and energy to develop the idea of setting up my own business.

This is when I came up with a definition of courage as it related to my own life. For me, courage is about believing in yourself enough so that you turn every obstacle around you into *windows of opportunity* - jumping in points from which you can learn and progress. My belief, my mindset, that I was going to make it no matter what I found ahead of me, empowered me to make this fairly risky decision.

I also believe that this courage actually blinded me from seeing the risk of failure. I was setting up a business in a country that was still developing. But, because I believed in myself so much, I was pretty oblivious to the specter of potential failure even though I had no capital.

Let me make it clear: my courage was not related to my business idea. My business ideas have changed so many times in the last 19 years, it's not funny. My courage was based on my ability and the confidence I had in myself that I could sell whatever services I chose to offer to the market—plain and simple, and no looking back.

It happens all around us. When you get hired at a company, you accept a job based not on what you already know about the job. You accept the job based on your abilities, and how you think you're going to perform. Not only that, but there are the expectations of the company that's hiring you. That creates more than a little pressure.

You don't accept the job because you believe so much in what you already know about the job requirement, or because of the brand/company that you're going to work for. If they have a stellar reputation, that, of course, helps build your confidence that much more. Ultimately, we assume things in our lives because we believe in our abilities to deliver.

For me, the fact that I was so oriented towards sales took me back once again to my first stepfather, the successful businessman. He was a businessman working with foreign companies. That was my first dream job, to become like him. Setting up my own business was living the dream that I had since the age of 10: to become a businessman.

There I was in 2000, at the age of 32, leaving my steady, lucrative job. But I wanted more. I wanted something of my own, something I could build and watch grow. So, I went about setting up my own company. This is how things started.

Courage Can Overcome Worry

Worry and anxiety are two of the biggest detriments to success in any endeavor. Staying in a constant state of high alert is not the answer. In fact, doing so will most assuredly prevent you from leading courageously, and create even more fearfulness within you. Allowing yourself to be enveloped by anxiety and worry robs you of focus and energy; it creates stress and fatigue and displaces any opportunity to experience joy and victory.

Studies have shown that some of primary things that cause people to worry center around events that never even take place, or past situations that cannot be changed. Other sources of worry have been revealed to be petty and unimportant, and only a minuscule percentage tend to be about things that can be shifted and/or controlled.

As a thought leader, directing your energy into seeking solutions for things that can be changed is a huge step in the right direction. Refusing to fritter away precious energy and time worrying about things that are static and unchangeable is another characteristic great leaders adopt. Taking action that is purposeful to create solutions with determination and zealousness is one sure way to thwart worry and employ a courage mindset to your best advantage.

The Courage Mindset Creates History and Inspiration

Nelson Mandela

Imprisoned for 27 years for his participation in political uprisings in opposition to the South African government, Nelson Mandela is one of the most stalwart and inspirational examples of someone who, no matter what, followed their courage mindset.

Being an anti-apartheid activist took tremendous courage. Even though that contributed to his arrest, once released, he resumed his work to end apartheid. He went on to become South Africa's first black president and to receive a Nobel Peace Prize. Due to his courage, leadership abilities, and undying commitment to create a better nation, South Africa's racial segregation was demolished, and now, multiracial elections take place.

A person with lesser courage might well have succumbed to the injustice and horrible conditions of his prison time, but Mandela found the strength within himself to emerge from that situation even stronger than before. The courage mindset can work wonders if one is willing to remain steadfast in their beliefs and life's mission. Nelson Mandela provided an exemplary case in point, making it through insurmountable odds to create a better life for his country.

Helen Keller

Definitely one of the most courageous people of all time, Helen Keller blazed trails where no one with disabilities had gone before. At just 19 months old, an illness left her blind and deaf. Keller's story continues to inspire generations, along with her shared journey with her beloved teacher, Anne Sullivan. The book about their journey together was adapted both into a stage and screenplay, *The Miracle Worker*.

Keller was the first deaf and blind person to graduate college with a Bachelor's degree. She authored several books and became a highly sought-after speaker worldwide. Her political views were considered radical in her day. She was a supporter and lecturer for many causes, including socialism, labor rights, women's suffrage, and more.

Keller's courage mindset kept her going until the age of 87. Her achievements are remarkable for any individual, let alone one who had such severe challenges to overcome. She defied the odds of her disability time and again, including writing twelve books, traveling to 35 countries, doing fundraising for the blind, and becoming an inductee into the National Women's Hall of Fame.

If you are seeking inspiration to keep going despite many challenges on your path, take a few minutes to reflect upon what Keller accomplished in her life, and take heart. You have more courage within you than you know. Her example can help you tap into it, and no matter what you face, courage can help you to reach your goals.

Courage and Confidence

When starting my first business, I had confidence. The confidence that I had was in myself. It wasn't so much confidence in the market, nor the idea that I wanted to create a Romanian business. This was a deeply rooted core confidence that blinded me, actually shielded me, from seeing potential adversity. This kept me from seeing the risk of not making it, and buying into that possibility. Also, my wife had a lot of faith in me that I was going to make it. All of these factors drove my decision to start my own business.

Courage is an innate drive. Really, the drive to succeed is a foundational piece, an accelerator, or a catalyst for the mindset. It's very important when we talk about the courage mindset. You must employ your courage mindset to challenge yourself to actually *live* your dreams.

Many people refuse to live their dreams, or to go after them because they don't have that drive. The fear of failure looms so large for them that they often give up and don't even try to realize their dreams. Their mindset seems to be, *If I never try, at least I won't fail.* This is sad, and one of my hopes is that my story will inspire others to breathe a fresh belief into their dreams, and to pursue those with all their heart and soul.

What was important to me at this turning point in my life was that in addition to having the drive, I felt like I was ready. I also felt that the moment was now because it was what I had been preparing for since my childhood. I didn't let the fact that I didn't have the capital to invest in the company stop me from proceeding with starting my own company in Romania.

The company's first computer was a black and white IBM received from my father-in-law. My business idea was not complete but was based on my previous needs as a student. When I graduated from the university, we had no gowns and caps to celebrate our graduation. This had never felt right to me, so I decided set up a company offering graduation services to high schools and universities - the first of its kind in Romania. I used the only money that I had at the time to order the first set of graduation gowns from the US.

I started working with the Romanian high schools and universities. It didn't take me long to realize that this was an extremely seasonal business, as graduation only happens once a year, in the same month. Also, getting many schools to organize the graduation events on different days in a short window of time was almost impossible. It was time to panic, but my drive kept me strong.

Then, I saw the opportunity to go into advertising and marketing services. More specifically, we began offering youth marketing services to multinational companies that provided products and services targeted to students. After all, we were the only company with official direct access to the schools, having already been approved by the Ministry of Education on one side and schools and universities on the other. So, that piece was in place.

With no money left, there were many days I worked with one employee. Typically, we didn't have money to buy lunch. When we did, we would stop at the corner store next to our office to buy a loaf of bread and some ham. It was all that I could afford. We were together all day, holding three to four meetings or calls at a time with potential clients. At the end of the day, we went home for dinner, but then came right back to the office in order to work at night, replying to clients' email requests and doing whatever else needed to be done.

Throughout all of these early development challenges, I still held onto the strong belief that things were going to work out. There was no other option in my mind. So, I kept on moving towards overcoming the obstacles that occurred and forged onward.

Defining Moments

My initial defining moment in business arrived with the first contract we got. This took place four months after launching our business idea of becoming an advertising and marketing agency. We were implementing a campaign for Chupa Chups. Those are lollipops. Chupa Chups' advertising agency saw a potential in our youth marketing positioning. They offered us the contract to see if we could deliver on our promises.

I remember we had to set up the details and logistics overnight, as we were such a young company with no procedures and no proper database of all the school details in the territory. In addition to normal work hours, we would come to work at night, from 10:00 p.m. until 2:00 a.m., building our databases and preparing presentations for clients.

My father-in-law, who lived in a city 370 miles from us, moved to Bucharest for a couple of months to help build the stepping-stones of my company, from working procedures to client meetings. It was far from easy to achieve everything, but we delivered.

Not long afterwards, we signed our first direct contract with a multinational company. That company was Unilever. We were going to implement a campaign in schools across Romania for one of their brands, Rexona. I saw that as a second moment of truth because it was adding up as more proof that my faith in setting up a business in Romania was justified.

After the first few years of operation, I decided to look abroad to search for partnerships I could bring into Romania. Shortly after I started my search on the Internet, I came across the US-based merchandising company, SPAR. At that time, they had several international partnerships. I seized the opportunity to approach them with the idea of entering the Romanian market. It took about a year to negotiate and set up the partnership.

It was an important moment for me. Looking at my background and where I was then, I perceived it as a great accomplishment that I was able to successfully negotiate a joint venture with a US-based company listed on NASDAQ.

Throughout the start-up of my business, my wife was working. So, when the company wasn't making any money, especially during the early years, she took care of all of our home expenses. As I would regularly run out of cash, I also had to borrow money from friends. As the saying goes, "A friend in need is a friend indeed." I enjoyed then and will always be grateful for the support of my best friends in those difficult times.

One of those friends was my best friend from Liberia, a former student I had met in Romania. By that time, he was living in the UK. We had stayed in touch, so I called him up and asked him for a loan of £3,000, which, of course, I repaid in due time. He is now in Liberia and is an excellent doctor. In fact, he is the doctor who currently takes care of my family back home.

We went on to work with other leading multinational companies, including Unilever, Procter & Gamble, Vodafone, Nespresso, L'Oreal, Coca-Cola, Kimberly Clark, McDonalds, and many more. Today, we have clients that are blue-chip companies. It all started with the confidence that I had in myself, and a drive that was so strong that it blinded me from seeing the risk of failure or any obstacle in my way. It all began from there.

I believed in myself, I had the drive, and I didn't see or worry about the obstacles that were going to come. Full disclosure: I have had lots of difficult moments since I started my business. But, I persisted, and I still do today.

An important piece here is knowing when you have nowhere to go back to, nothing to fall back on, and are past the point of no return. I believe that people who eventually quit down the road are those who have also left their options open. But, me? I burned my bridges. I burned away the possibility of reconnecting with all of my previous options when I made my decision to go into business. I just didn't leave any other options open. I gave myself no other choice than to succeed, period.

In life, when you make a decision to do something, and you're not 100 percent sure, you end up leaving to pursue other options. In Napoleon Hill's timeless book *Think and Grow Rich,* he shares the story of a general whose division went sailing across the sea to an island to fight the enemy. When they got off the ship, he told his soldiers to burn down the boat. He said by looking back and seeing that they now had no point of return, they knew beyond the shadow of a doubt that they must either win or perish.

That's the mindset you need when you decide to do something. You know that there is no point of return. That's what I think the courage mindset implies. It's knowing that you will overcome everything that stands in the way of your success. Knowing that you refuse to be disappointed if obstacles pop up in your way, or when you encounter difficulties. The word *quit* is simply not an option.

The fact that I eliminated all these options contributed to my courage to stay in business in Romania. I could have always quit, closed down my company and applied for a job. But, I didn't see that as an option. My drive is to continuously overcome the difficulties that I encounter, outmaneuver any obstacles, and move on.

If I look back and ask myself, "Where did I get all this bravery? Where did this courage come from?" I think it has to do with being born in a poverty- stricken village as a poor child. I believe if you look at where you were born, the environment, roots, and all of that, your bravery, courage or drive can often be traced back to those things. Depending on what conditions you were born into, as well as how you were brought up, can affect your mindset.

Doubt

I had moments of doubt my entire life. Anyone who tries to tell you they've never felt a doubt in their life - well, let's say that's probably far from the truth. I felt responsible for giving up the comfort of a steady job while pursuing my dream and at the expense of the financial stability I would have loved to offer to my family. I felt responsible for running a sustainable business that was providing work to hundreds of full-time employees and part-time employees every month. I knew a lot of people depended on me, especially while going through the harsh periods.

So, with that many commitments, like many people, I had and still have doubts. It's part of being human. But, I always return to my courage mindset to stay focused and committed.

I tell you all this so you know that no matter how successful you are, you will always need courage. Things can change overnight as many of the events in my life show. But, with a courage mindset, it is possible to meet them head on and not just survive but thrive.

Steps to Integrate the Courage Mindset into Your Daily Life

1. **Learn to trust yourself.** You do this by creating small successes along the way. It's a lifestyle, not just a skill.

2. **Keep a journal of your successes.** Write down your decisions and how you arrived at them. You can keep them in your head, but having them on paper lets you go back and review them and track your progress.

3. **Write down your failures.** Thousands of organizations around the world conduct debriefings after every mission, project, success, or failure. These reviews take a cold, hard look at what went right and what went wrong. This allows the organizations to create policies and procedures, train their employees, and develop a courage mindset. Even if you don't have staff or others you can debrief with, it's important to analyze your failures. You can't improve what you can't measure.

4. **Strengthen your courage muscles.** Courage is like a muscle: you must use it frequently and increase the demand on yourself daily if you want your courage to grow. If you have children, you know how they explore their world, a small piece at a time.

They may crawl first, then walk, but at some point, they make the leap and start opening cabinets and getting into everything, oblivious to whether it will hurt them or not. They have started to develop their courage muscles, and will keep doing so unless they start listening to their parents say, "No! That will hurt you," or "No, that's bad." Sadly, many of us still listen to those voices even after we are grown. But, you can still build those muscles.

5. **Step out of your comfort zone in small ways to begin building your courage.** Travel, try a new food, go to a new restaurant - learn something that scares you, whether it's a new hobby or a new skill. Each time you step out of your comfort zone and try something that scares you, or at least makes you nervous and uncomfortable, you train your brain to be courageous.

Fear has a bad reputation because it is uncomfortable. No one likes to be fearful, except maybe people who enjoy horror movies. But many successful people feel fear every day. The difference is, they've learned to use fear. Popular speakers, pilots, attorneys, and entrepreneurs all experience fear every day. But rather than let fear dictate their actions, or force them to walk away from a situation, they use fear as a tool. What is their fear telling them? Instead of listening, they choose to control and use their fear, so it won't control and use them.

06 THE PERSISTENCE MINDSET

"If you can't fly, then run. If you can't run, then walk. If you can't walk then crawl, but whatever you do, you have to keep moving forward."
—Dr. Martin Luther King, Jr.

This quote embodies the fiber of persistence and perseverance. Having a persistence mindset requires that you seek the next best approach when something doesn't go according to plan. Make the best of the options available to you and move forward towards your goals rather than abandoning your mission.

Everyone faces obstacles along their path in life. The difference is that some people choose to forge onward rather than allowing challenges to stop them in their tracks. I had my share of obstacles, and because I chose to keep going, to do everything I could to overcome them, it made me stronger. That is something I have never regretted.

Sometimes you feel as though you simply cannot go on, especially after being faced with a domino effect, or landslide of one challenge after another. That's normal, perfectly human. Yet, there is something deep within you, an inner strength that can rise to the surface and inspire and encourage you to move forward despite all odds.

Think about those times in your life when this has been the case, and know that same persistence and resilience is there for you, always. It may be that you simply need to come at a situation from a new perspective, a new approach. It certainly does not mean you must abandon a goal or project altogether. I will share some of my personal experiences in the hope that you take heart about your own, and persist.

Test of Faith

Along the way, I went through bankruptcy. It's normal to have fears in life. The fear of failing is one of the modern-day obstacles that stops millions, if not billions, of people from going after their dreams. What I think we should fear most is accepting failure as the end of the route to our dreams or goals.

As entrepreneurs, when we feel we lose control, we can try to avoid failure by seeking professional help or hiring top professionals to assist us in running our businesses. Still, there is no guarantee that we won't fail. In our personal lives, we can follow a safe path. But again, there is no assurance that challenges will not come our way. That's what life really is, isn't it? Life's a series of ups and downs, akin to a roller coaster ride, at times.

During my 19 years as an entrepreneur and innovative investor, I have made many poor investments, resulting in losses of more than half a million dollars. This also involved going through bankruptcy with one of my businesses. At the early start of the bankruptcy proceedings, we borrowed money from a friend to invest in the retail business. Unable to pay back our debt and without any other sources of financing, we were forced to sell our home and repay the money owed. Yes, it was extremely painful, but I did not allow this experience to stop me from dreaming big and continuing to work hard to achieve the goals I had set for myself and my family.

My bankruptcy procedures lasted for more than three years. It involved the banks, creditors/suppliers, the state, and my former partners. At the request of my former partners, after my breakout from the business relationship with them, I was investigated by the Department for Anti-Fraud in Romania.

The initial stage of the investigation involved the anti-fraud officers interrogating me several times at their headquarters. For the record, that building was intimidating, actually, quite frightening in appearance. It had very small rooms, with almost no air circulating, and no proper lighting system. I was not served any water or given any accommodation whatsoever. It felt like walking into a prison. The investigation extended into my personal life as well as the firm's financial records.

The officers individually questioned most of my employees as part of the investigation, almost closing down my other businesses altogether. This initial stage of the investigation lasted more than six months. At the end of it all, the Department for Anti-Fraud found no evidence to support the claims brought against me by my former partners.

The whole bankruptcy situation felt earth-shattering to me. It unfolded incredibly quickly, so much so that at times I didn't know what was happening around me. I used to tremble and sweat each time I was called to the Anti-Fraud headquarters, not knowing what to expect. But, somehow, at the end of it, I found a way to look at all of those trials and tribulations as actually being a great part of my business experience. Why? Because I learned everything that I could from it.

Writing about all of this now feels almost surreal. In retrospect, it seems like I have a protective mechanism that keeps all past negative events out of my head. I certainly don't dwell on them. They are only triggered when I am reminded of those times by others asking questions or interviewing me about my past. I am proud that I have this system of mindsets in me because it has helped me to let go of all my past struggles and challenges. I hope sharing my story may in some way teach others how to do the same.

Don't live in the past - live in the present. That is what matters most.

Periods of Rework

Reworking something involves making changes to bring something up-to-date. It involves reinventing, improving, and/or optimizing. Reworking a business following a financial setback involves assessing what caused the setback, and then creating and implementing a plan to move forward. It's also an opportunity to rethink your original business model, define its core as well as the key processes that worked and didn't work, compute profits, cut losses, and then, move on.

My first rework call was when I was faced with terminating the joint venture with SPAR, the US-based merchandising company. Losing this joint venture meant a huge financial loss, as I had invested heavily in this project, and counted on it to get my business to the next level. For complex reasons, it didn't work at that time. After the joint venture termination, I was left with a fragmented business, a negative cash flow, huge debts, and a severe lack of available working capital for my advertising company.

The only valuable asset I had left was my team. I had formed a very strong team, which I consider to be the most highly prized non-financial working capital that any company can hope to have. My team shared my values, mindsets, involvement, and level of commitment to success.

Even in the face of seemingly overwhelming odds, I started negotiations with P&G, which proved to be a real turning point. It had taken me more than three years of calling on them annually before I was able to book an appointment. I was calling them in order to present my agency, our services, and what we could contribute to their business.

Every year they answered that they would get back to me when they needed my services. But, every year, I called upon them two or three times to present again what we had to offer, and they always gave the same answer. It didn't stop me. It didn't discourage me because I refused to give up.

I steadfastly continued pursuing them in this way until one pivotal day when they called on us to discuss a possible collaboration. It took another three or four months before we got our first contract signed with P&G. But, it was well worth the wait and persistence. From that point forward, we have been acknowledged on the market as an agency that companies like P&G came to when they needed marketing services in Romania. As I said, it was a turning point. All of this was possible because I believed and I persisted.

Although we were a small agency at that time, we did prove to be a strong one. We embraced the challenges, thereby showing the true value of our team and our togetherness. We had a conjoined dedication to success and were not about to accept anything less. It didn't matter to us about the unknown, even though we had no idea of what to expect from P&G at the beginning. What really mattered for my team was doing business with this top world-class company. We shared a great deal of excitement and pride for having them as our client.

P&G took us through months of business evaluation. They carefully vetted our team, business competences and more. All of this happened before the first contract was signed and negotiations started. During these months, I recall discussing with a client business ethics, transparency, accountability, dedication, flexibility, cost efficiency, financial audits, and many other business aspects for the first time.

All of these powerful values were already instilled in us as a team and were an innate part of our makeup. Therefore, we owned the essence of what a major player and plum client like P&G was looking for on the market. It had been our way of doing business from the time the company was set up, and that was the inner mindset; essentially, the mission statement of our team.

From the very beginning of our collaboration, we learned a lot from the P&G team. The negotiation process was a win-win for every party.

We learned how to properly calculate the agency's overheads during that period, as well as how to more effectively negotiate with our suppliers. Transparency was a key factor, whether it was about calculating costs, in reporting, or always staying in proper communication with the P&G team.

An article by Andreea Mindrila on the online news site ZF Live conveys the magnitude of our business with the P&G: "In times of crisis, Wave Division doubled its business, reaching 4.8 million euros last year."[6]

Nearly eight years later, our partnership came to an end, forcing me into the second rework of my business. The loss of P&G was devastating. With a huge part of our turnover coming from P&G, to say losing them as a client was difficult, is a gross understatement.

The entire company had developed the P&G way of thinking and doing business during our years of collaboration. The P&G way of managing business was entirely different from our previous day-to-day way of doing business on the market.

---

[6] [https://www.zf.ro/auxiliar/in-vreme-de-criza-wave-division-si-a-dublat-afacerile-ajungand-anul-trecut-la-4-8-milioane-euro-10261675]

The immediate challenge after the loss of P&G was reworking the processes inside the company. I was once again faced with redesigning the agency: the team, mindsets, and cash flow management. To top it off, of course, the most difficult part was winning new clients.

Another challenge that arose was that people left the agency, which actually I expected would happen. As the first evaluation stage before setting sail on the boat, I needed to find out who was still on board.

The rework of Wave Division after the loss of P&G was based on the prudent financial policies of the past years. We had put aside a sufficiently large reserve so that we could financially support ourselves. This was a huge blessing that sustained us during the time it took to rebalance the agency's client portfolio.

Famous Entrepreneurs Who Persisted

I want to mention a couple of examples of well-known entrepreneurs who faced rejection and multiple challenges, yet, by using the persistence mindset, they triumphed.

Warren Buffet

It's fairly commonly known that Harvard Business School rejected Warren Buffet when he was a young man. His father's undying faith in Warren's abilities, as well as his own self-confidence and persistence, led to his acceptance at Columbia. There, he worked with some experts in investing who influenced the foundation for Berkshire Hathaway. Although Berkshire Hathaway has morphed into a multi-billion dollar company over the years, in its infancy, it suffered some failure. But, Buffet again persisted. He has said that all such challenges and setbacks wound up improving his life and helped him transform barriers into favorable outcomes.

Arianna Huffington

No stranger to the persistence mindset, Arianna Huffington received rejections from nearly forty publishers before her second book went into print. Rather than ditching her manuscript, she kept pushing onward and turned the rejections into fuel and motivation to reach her goal of getting published.

When she first founded the Huffington Post in 2005, it was not well received. In fact, its critics ripped into it, citing a lack of quality. Essentially, they scoffed at it, dismissed it, and figured it would go belly up in short order. However, Huffington persisted, and the Post worked its way up to more than a billion pages of views per year by 2011, at which time AOL purchased it for $315 million.

Finding the best platform and the right marketplace to pave the road to success often requires persistence. Refusing to take *no* for an answer is also another key component of the persistence mindset. Huffington is no stranger to either, and her example can serve to inspire you to carry on, no matter what challenges crop up in your endeavors.

Steps to Integrate the Persistence Mindset into Your Daily Life

1. **Find someone or something that inspires you and follow or refer to them often.** Inspiration can be videos on YouTube, a book, a mentor, a colleague, your spouse/partner, or even a religious practice. But, you need something or someone to turn to when you are feeling depressed, scared, or panicked. Anytime you feel that you just don't have what it takes to keep going, turn to one of these

sources of inspiration to build yourself back up, and persevere.

My wife is a tremendous source of inspiration for me every day. I also turn to books, videos, and stories of other people who have triumphed over adversity. If they can do it, then so can I.

2. **Ignore the voices around you.** Every day there are voices around you. Naysayers will wear you down, spouting things such as, "You can't do that. You can't do this. You're going to fail." Eliminate all of those voices.

For example, I've been telling some friends that I'm writing a book. One of their first questions typically is, "What's wrong with you? Are you mad? What are you going to do with a book in Romania?" I have what they don't have: the vision to see that a book isn't limited to a single country's market. Granted, my *agency* or business is limited to the Romanian market in a way. But, in terms of a market for *readers* who want to understand how to succeed? A book like that has no limitations.

Blocking, ignoring, or refusing to entertain those negative voices, those fear-mongers, is one thing that you can do to remove the greatest discouragement from pursuing your dreams. Negative people and voices are dream stealers, if you allow them to be. So, don't allow them! Persevere and keep moving forward.

3. **Don't be afraid to try, and try again**. Yes, there are many theories about calculated risks. But, you can make the best decisions, take the safest risks, and still fail. You can make the worst decisions, take the most insane risks, and succeed. Either way, what will be, will be. You can hire all the experts around you that you want. God knows I have hired so many people in this company that I thought were going to do the work for me. I thought they were all my solutions. But, until I tried, I didn't know that I was wrong.

Muster up your perseverance and try with all your might - even if that means failing. The good news is this: you'll learn more from your failures than your successes, so consider every failure a lesson in what to do differently next time. That's how experts become experts: they only know what works and doesn't work because they have failed so many times they are intimately familiar with what will work and what won't. No one ever learned a great life lesson by throwing in the towel and quitting. Most people who quit before pulling out all the stops possible often spend much of the rest of their life wondering, *what if?*

4. **Find good people and keep them in your life.** You need people. I'm still in business because I opened my heart to the people around me. I'm not judged by my mistakes and failures. Associate yourself with the right people. They will empower you to have the courage to be brave, to follow your dreams and your ideas.

5. **Realize that failure is not permanent.** *Failure is a situation that happens, not a permanent condition.* Failure is a place on your path, not your path itself. You will fail every day in various areas of your life, but you likely don't call it failure, but rather a mistake. Why should you be afraid to try? Because you're going to make a mistake? That's wrong. Try. If you fail, you will learn something valuable. If you succeed, you will gain more time to eventually fail, but more importantly, learn.

THE LEGACY MINDSET

"Life is a roller coaster of highs, lows, hard lefts, hard rights, and even some loop-de-loops. But, know this participation is mandatory as your legacy is the accumulation of what you gave back not what you took out."
—Donovan Nelson Butler, Master Sergeant U.S. Army

In its basic meaning, a legacy is a bequest, something of value transmitted by a predecessor or from the past. In its broader use, a legacy refers to one's accomplishments or ethics one will be remembered for after they pass away. However, there is something called a "living legacy" that has emerged and become important to many, especially I would say, for those age 40 and older. Those who value the importance of giving something of value to others, especially to younger generations.

The living legacy means that people's legacies grow and change as they do. I would say it's very contemporary, very real for today. You get the opportunity to share your knowledge and experiences NOW prior to your exit from this earth. Your legacy is your contribution, your value added to the world.

The point with the living legacy is exactly that; it is even more beneficial if one can offer his or her hard-earned wisdom *before* one passes on. To this end, the living legacy is my model for this mindset.

I have reached my legacy mindset by being aware of the chances I got throughout my life and trying with all my heart to give it back now, today, as often as possible. To this end, I seek constantly to contribute to the well-being and success of others.

The way I see it, the heart of a legacy mindset is about always putting people first, from those who are close to you, like your extended family and friends, to your colleagues and members of your community. It's about what you can do for others. It's about paying your *time*, *treasures*, *talents* and *thoughts* forward whenever someone thinks of you. It's always the beginning, not the past.

Sometimes, living my legacy has required making sacrifices. Sometimes, I put the needs of others ahead of my own, and even the needs of other people before my family as well. As a result, at times I may have made decisions to help others in ways that would negatively affect my family. This is one of my weaknesses. To be truthful with myself, I have to acknowledge my vulnerability. But somehow this, too, is part of my living legacy. So, there is nothing to hide. Our responsibility, of course, is to our own family first, because they are our primary support. We cannot fill the cups of others if we don't first fill our own cup. Here, our own cup represents a commitment to focusing on family first, whenever we can.

Becoming Aware of My Legacy Mindset

When I was growing up, living with my stepfather, G. Marcus Kelley, we had a quote on our wall. It said, "I shall pass this way but once. Therefore, any good that I can do or any kindness that I can show, let me do it now for I shall not pass this way again."

This was prominently displayed on the walls of the embassy, as well as the wall of our home. This quote defined *his* legacy. He lived his life always doing good for others, always showing kindness. His life was dedicated to being of service. It has influenced me as an adult. It's the reason why I focus my legacy mindset on putting people first.

One example of him living the people-first legacy was the fact that at the embassy in Romania, his policy was to always have an open house for all students from Liberia; in fact, for all foreign students. As I shared earlier, he became a father figure to them. Students came in whenever they finished their courses at university. They came for a safe shelter, a hot meal, and a chance to socialize with other students in their circumstances.

At most embassies, you have to stand outside and wait. This was our private residence where normally the public would not be invited. But, because of my father's policy, our residence was an open house. The Liberian community and those Liberian students became part of our family. My father never refused to do good for anyone.

At the residence, we were having a very difficult time as the war unfolded. Funding for the mission was no longer available, and the debts began to add up day by day and month after month. Being with my stepfather throughout this period, I got to understand him even much more than before, and

THE DRIVE TO AIM HIGH

I was able to grasp the deep meaning of his legacy mindset.

I got to understand his reason for remaining in Romania until the very last moment, even thought he could have left for the United States at any given time. He chose to stay in order to ensure that all the Liberian students were taken care of and had the support they needed to leave Romania upon their graduation. His staff was also still there, and as head of the mission, he couldn't see himself leaving without ensuring safe passage for all of them.

The very meaning of the legacy mindset for my stepfather was people first, which for him was more important than his own well-being. This somehow rubbed off on me. From the very start of my business, my entire company has been built around a people first philosophy.

Leadership Legacy

I was lucky to have been surrounded by the right people at the beginning of my business. It helped me go through some of the difficulties that confronted me in Romania. This falls under the legacy mindset, because our success in business – or failure – depends greatly on the people around us. We might be around people who criticize if we fail, or those who fall into the opposite category, who encourage us to move forward. Part of my *people first philosophy* is having the right people around you, those who lift you up when your spirits are down or celebrate your accomplishments with you.

Mihaela, my first employee, has been with the company for 19 years, since I first started the business in Romania. She was a part-time collaborator, working with me to answer telephones and helping with whatever needed to be done around the office. To be honest, I didn't even have an office at that point! We worked out of a room owned by the friend of a friend. It was an extremely old building, but the rent was next to nothing, so we couldn't beat the price.

Mihaela was student at that time in her third year of university. When she completed her studies, she continued working for me. She was promoted several times in the company, working her way up from account manager to client service manager. She later became the CEO and Partner of Wave Division, the company that I run now.

My operational director, Elena, has been within the company for 17 years. She also started as a part-time collaborator, going through various positions within the agency. I am grateful to have her beside me, challenging and supporting me for so many years.

The point here is that there is great value in investing in your employees to create long-term employee relationships. This is so good for everyone, including your customers. There is no question this is about spending time to build a powerful collaborative environment. As leaders, we should be helping others learn and grow, and also enabling them to embrace challenges without the fear of failure.

Another piece of the legacy mindset is forming partnerships with other like-minded people so that you can have more impact. Find and partner with others who have the same or a similar legacy mindset to yours. Think of the good that you can do! It isn't either/or. It's either you do it yourself - the Lone Ranger mentality - or you can build a network of others, teammates and coworkers with whom your conjoined wisdom then can spread over to other influencers. This is true because there is strength in numbers, and added value to your insights when you work together.

This perspective is about shifting from a local view - city, state, country - to a greater, grander worldview. Your insights can be valuable to people. The legacy mindset is one that includes not only you reaching down, pulling people up and then encouraging them to impact their peers, but also reaching out to other influencers and co-creating through collaboration.

The legacy mindset also includes mentoring whenever possible. People are more awake in Europe around this idea that "60 is the new 40" and that people are living longer. They are still very vibrant, so they figure they have a good two decades or more ahead of them. This unique time gives them the opportunity to mentor others. Mentoring in one's later years is such a powerful time because you're not in the beginning mode of your career. You've hit your stride. You're able to make a bigger difference in the world because you have more to offer.

When I reflect upon the issues that I have confronted in my career, I see that individuals usually focus on achieving growth for themselves, first. This is normal, but I believe a wider approach is needed. Achievers, like myself and perhaps like you, want to develop quickly. Achievers also want the rewards that come from their efforts as soon as possible. As leaders, achievers are mostly geared towards how profitable our businesses can become. But, placing profitability foremost rather than taking a *people first* approach can actually harm your business potential at the end of the day.

When we lost P&G, our major client who was contributing to a huge portion of our revenues, I had a decision to make. I could have reduced the company personnel by firing a significant number of them, but I didn't do that. Instead, I focused on reducing costs and optimizing our business processes. I did everything possible to keep everyone in the company until we could get another client that would replace the lost revenue. I put people first because of my legacy mindset.

The outcome was that our revenues almost doubled in 2018 compared to 2017. We continued to offer thousands of jobs yearly for students entering the job market in Romania. Since the incorporation of Wave Division, our contribution as an advertising agency has been creating a positive impact in forming the next generation's workforce.

By thinking only of how much profit we are going to make, or as individuals, how quickly we can grow, we often forget the importance of meaningful relationships in our workplace with our extended families. These are some of the issues that I think we are confronted with today when we contemplate the legacy mindset. It simply doesn't exist in so many people around us.

Family Responsibility Legacy

In Africa, we have a tradition where the big man in a family takes care of the little ones. I'm the big man of my family. I'm not the oldest because I have a brother who is two years older than I, but I'm the most educated. I have this responsibility to care about and to help my family as a way of living my legacy.

It's about deep values instilled in me since my first years spent in my village. Values transmitted through generations in the place I came from. I'm the most educated person in my family; therefore, it's my obligation to somehow embrace this legacy mindset. It's not just my responsibility, but my honor *to give back*, to support my family in order for the little ones to become educated for the betterment of their future.

Whatever your culture is, however your "village" or family is structured, think about ways you can help its members reach their goals in realistic ways. Think about schooling, tutoring, parenting, emotional, and even appropriate financial support. Sometimes your legacy mindset will include setting boundaries and saying *no*. But, the end goal will always be to help that person, family member, or community member become better in some way.

Steps to Integrate the Legacy Mindset into Your Daily Life

1. **Identify three positive things your family has said that you have contributed to them.** For example, take one of my colleagues, Alice. She tried this exercise and discovered her family saw her as the one to turn to for organizing parties, the person they relied upon when they wanted to brainstorm new meal options (she is a great cook), and the only one they would count on to help them with any things they needed to write, whether it was a new resume, a blog post, or even a cool tweet on social media. After taking this inventory inside her family, Alice felt more purposeful. It also opened up ideas for her as to how to help others *outside* of her family, such as volunteering to help a

couple of local nonprofits that could benefit from her talents.

2. **Create a legacy journal.** This exercise only requires a simple lined journal where you start to take note of the things you admire in your family members. This journal can include your insights and positive impressions of your siblings, children, spouse, parents, and even cousins with whom you are close. This legacy journal will hopefully be a treasured gift from you to your family.

Note that you can also create a legacy journal for your organization where you share, in writing (something I believe will become more valuable as we continue to be computer-centric), your thoughts on the many intangible gifts of kindness, creativity, leadership, and more from your employees and vendor partners. This journal can be the corporate diary of your workplace that celebrates all the good things others have done for you and your company throughout the year.

3. **Create a legacy program for your employees, customers, or clients.** This can be something as simple as supporting your local schools by having your employees provide mentoring to students.

You can also establish a scholarship, or internships at your company where you focus on helping students.

4. **Think about how your company impacts current employees.** While I have several employees who have been with me for decades, the days of people staying with a company more than a year or two is becoming rarer, at least in the US. Think about how you can shape your company's culture and how you treat your employees from day one to their departure. How can you use that time, however long it is, to instill a people first legacy in their lives? It might be part of your official policies, or through company meetings, conferences, and gatherings (employee picnics and holiday celebrations, and so on), or maybe the company shuts down for three days to a week to allow time for employees, along with their families, to attend a conference or event together.

08 WHY MINDSET MATTERS

The seven mindsets I have presented in this book are God-given to you, no matter your place of birth, education, or race. Discipline and hard work are required to master these mindsets. I encourage you to embrace hard work and discipline as you employ them, for this is how you shall succeed.

Complete Circle: Family Values

I reunited with my birth parents after a long separation of 25 years. I didn't even know if they were alive; yet, I had a strong belief that they were. I knew I had to do all I could to find them, so I booked a trip to Liberia.

With help from a good friend, a former Liberian student in Romania, I found my village, which I remembered well from my childhood. There, I found my mom.

Just imagine. I left my village at the age of ten. But, almost as though time had stood still, I swiftly walked to the house where I was born. A quarter of a century had passed. I didn't even know if my parents were alive; yet, I knew where I was born, and that this was my house.

When I arrived in front of the house, I saw her. There stood my mother sweeping the porch.

"Hello, Mom," I said.

She looked at me, and asked, "Who are you?"

I answered, "I'm your son, Allieu (my given name)."

She replied, "Who gave you the right to say you're my son?"

I replied calmly, "Because I am your son."

"If you're my son, tell me something about you or about me."

She had the nerve to give me a quiz, after not hearing from me for 25 years, if you can imagine that. She felt the truth of whom I was, but she couldn't believe I was standing there in front of her. But, all of a sudden, she did realize it was me. She fell to the ground crying. Words don't adequately describe the waves of feelings I was experiencing at that moment. There had been doubts at various points along my life's path, but I never lost sight of one of my dearest goals: to find my birth parents in order to provide for them and make them proud.

It was so satisfying to connect with my parents again. I couldn't imagine what they had endured or what they thought or felt during all those years that I was gone.

When you are born with many options, I think the amount of bravery, courage, or whatever you choose to call it, might not be the same. We are all born with a mindset that holds great potential. But, what we achieve in life depends on how burning our desire is to succeed. The mindsets you need to achieve success will be revealed to you – if you choose to be open to see them. These mindsets are needed on your path, and you can embrace them if you expect them, look for them, and don't lose sight of your dreams.

In my case, I grew up with a mindset that saw potential. I needed to be a better man. I needed to see the better part of life. Since reuniting with my parents, I have completed the circle, the one that began with my mother telling me at very young age that I was to "become a big man." My story is not over, but just continuing as I strive to grow without ceasing, and as I work and rework my life and business, so I can continue doing what I love.

Lessons of Life

During my journey, I have consciously developed these mindsets, without acknowledging them until later in life. I have also had the benefit of seeing my family employing them in ways far beyond what I thought was possible.

I saw my stepfather G. Marcus Kelley espousing the Persistence Mindset during the Liberian Civil War and living his Legacy Mindset throughout his life. My in-laws in Romania have shown the Persistence and Resilience Mindsets, further displaying through their actions that age and human limitations can't stop you from staying true to your dream, even when you are faced with provocation, disruption, and sorrow.

Then, there is my son, who at a very young age, demonstrated the Passion Mindset as he committed to the constant rigor and training it takes to realize his dream of becoming a world class tennis player.

Yes, it's true that past experiences, environment, culture, and other events in your life might or might not trigger you to access these seven mindsets. But, this doesn't mean you can't master them.

So, ask yourself:

- How can I usher them into my life tomorrow?

- How will I start putting them to use?

- How can I further tap into them to become the best *me* possible?

There is no secret formula for using these mindsets. The important thing is to start now.

As Napoleon Hill once stated, "There is one quality which one must possess to win, and that is definiteness of purpose, the knowledge of what one wants, and a burning desire to possess it."

Some people might choose to argue that what one is exposed to in their upbringing creates their mindsets, rather than those being an inherent part of each individual. I believe the truth lies somewhere between the two.

From my personal experience, I believe by employing the Observation Mindset (the first one I began developing as a child), all the way through the other six mindsets, they created in me a willingness to also consider the mindsets of others. This openness to learn constantly then led to me deciding what mindset fit into the design of my life's path. Many times, these mindsets have inspired me to approach my life-plan from very different angles. As a result, I am constantly learning new ways of looking at life, ways that have helped me *lead* instead of always following the lead of others.

The mindset lessons are available to all of us in our lives. We are surrounded by opportunities on a daily basis. But, it is up to us whether we take the time to evaluate the potential benefits of applying one or more of the seven mindsets to each situation/opportunity. I have come to believe that focusing on the best possible case scenario will lead to the wisest choices. All of the mindsets join forces to influence those choices. When you focus on what you *do* want to achieve rather than entertaining any negative aspects of what you do *not* want, then you stay truer to your own desires and goals. You will see the beneficial results of your efforts when you look back at the positive outcomes that resulted from your decisions.

But, in order for you to put these seven mindsets to work for you, you must have a strong belief in yourself and your purpose. Tapping into the power of the mindsets also calls for a commitment and the drive to work hard along with a burning desire for success. Success, without the hard work, isn't going to come simply by believing.

For me, as mentioned at the beginning of this book, it was the everlasting impact of my mother's words; those words she repeated to me as a child. Honoring those words drove me to discover the seven mindsets and then to develop them along the way and access them as needed.

It was no easy walk for me, but I successfully overcame each obstacle I faced because I refused to see failure as the end route to my dream.

All was made possible because of my determination to aim high, coupled with learning and leveraging the seven mindsets.

THIS BUSINESS CALLED LIFE: CONNECTING THE SEVEN MINDSETS

Now let's focus on connecting the seven mindsets and then utilizing them to reach your full potential. Who are you?

Who you are doesn't refer to who you are currently. It also refers to the "you" that you have become as a result of the journey you have taken. Your journey includes where you started from all the way to where you are at this particular moment. It's also about your family, relatives, and friends, peers and so on. By using the Observation Mindset, you can reflect on all of the many good and bad experiences you have been through.

In my case, I used this mindset to track the growth points I experienced along my journey. I observed that I overcame hurdles such as my delayed education, the lack of "guidance" on the part of my birth parents as well as the lack of a balanced and steady environment during my childhood. But, I also observed that the combined challenges presented to me only made me want to fight and succeed more instead of bringing me to my knees.

What's Next?

You *create* your life day by day, year by year. Once you have begun using the mindset exercises I've offered in this book, you will soon find your life improving.

Each one of the mindsets here is a tool for you to change your life in powerful ways. I shared my personal stories with you because they were the ones that I had reflected on the most and, as such, provided the insights I needed to attain my goals. Any time you tap into your own personal journey and the stories that evolve from it, you are better able to make choices that are more powerful and successful. More importantly, I hope you are able to see a process in the stories and that they can inspire you to grow your own powerful mindsets. Mine took me from a young boy with absolutely nothing, who had little hope of ever realizing even a modest lifestyle, to today being someone who has been able to attain success.

Truly effective leaders ask for feedback regularly, and then act on it. They take input provided by mentors, coaches and team members and put it into action. These leaders also engage in regular self-reflection. This involves being open. Begin now, rather than waiting another day. Start today on the path to your own success through the mindsets I have shared. But the best news is that you don't have to learn alone.

Visit my Mindset Bonus Page at www.al-kamara.com/bonus now to get free tools to benefit even more from the 7 Mindsets. Here you will not only get the kind of inspiration you can use to attain your dreams, but you will also become part of my community of support. Why? None of us does it alone. If it weren't for the wonderful, charitable, and gracious mentors I had throughout my life, I would not be here sharing my story and insights.

Because I've been blessed to be helped by a number of amazing mentors, I now can help you. Won't you join me?

Here's to your success!

BEFORE YOU GO

It was such as honor to spend time with you throughout your reading of this book. I'd like to take just a few more minutes to make a request. It is not a large one.

If you enjoyed this book, would you be so kind as to take a moment, go to Amazon, look up the title, *The Drive to Aim High*, and leave a short review? Even if you only had time to go through a couple of chapters you will be able to leave a review and, if you desire, go back later and add to it once you've had a chance to complete the book. Your first impressions are very useful, so don't worry if you have only time now to review one or two chapters.

Finally, note that books succeed by the kind, generous time readers take to leave honest reviews. This is how other readers learn about books that are most beneficial for them to buy. To this end, I thank you in advance for this very kind gesture of appreciation. It means the world to me.

ACKNOWLEDGEMENTS

To say this book is mine is overstated. It belongs to all of those people who have contributed to my life, from the beginning of my journey in my tiny village near Monrovia, Liberia.

My life long journey would not have been completed without my wife and two children, Brindusa, Patrick and Philip. Thank you for making the book within me become alive, after so many years of living it.

To my step-parents, for their contributions towards my education and making me the person I am today - Alphonso B. Gaye, the late Minnie Louise Greene, and my beloved stepfather, the late G. Marcus Kelley.

My team at Wave Division, the journey of a leader is always long, but even longer without a team. Mihaela, Elena, Oana, you guys rock!

To my publisher, editor and writing coach, Melissa G Wilson, and her team at Networlding Publishing, thanks for the wonderful work. I enjoyed every moment of our work together. Can't wait for us to begin working on my next book.

Last, but not least, to my brother Mustapha Kamara. We both are now the big men of our family in Liberia. Thank you for your support!

Printed in Poland
by Amazon Fulfillment
Poland Sp. z o.o., Wrocław